1.25

CHRIST HEALING

CHRIST HEALING

BY THE

Rev. E. HOWARD COBB, M.A.

Late Warden of the Home of Divine Healing, Crowhurst
Rector of Waddington, Lincs, 1911–20
Vicar of Mill Hill, Middlesex, 1920–28
Rector of Crowhurst, Sussex, 1928–30

"As many as touched Him were
made perfectly whole."

ST. LUKE'S PRESS

ST. LUKE'S PRESS
40 Myrtle Avenue¡
Irvington
N.J. 07111

This paperback edition 1975

Printed in Great Britain by
Hunt Barnard Printing Ltd, Aylesbury, Bucks.

PREFACE

THE first object of this book is to attempt to show that the healing of body and mind by the Grace of God is in accordance with the teaching of Holy Scripture, and is just as real as in the days of our Lord's Ministry on earth. The second purpose is to help those who believe, to find this Healing through prayer and faith, and the Ministry of the Church.

I prefer to call this healing "Divine Healing," rather than "Spiritual" or "Faith" Healing, because the word "Spiritual" is apt to be confused with "Spiritism"; and "Faith" might imply faith in oneself rather than in God. The Healing I am describing is purely the life-giving power of God, overcoming disease and building up new strength. Human beings may be used as channels, either in the way of prayer or personal ministration; but the Healing is from God, through Jesus Christ, and from Him alone.

If I have made statements which are not strictly in accordance with generally accepted belief, I suggest that they should be tested by careful examination of the Scriptures, which should prove more convincing than the claim of any authority in support of them.

There are several cases of healing mentioned in the various chapters, and it has been suggested that they would have more weight if I were to quote medical testimony to their reality. This, however, would be contrary to the spirit of the book, which is to encourage faith in the promises of God.

I do not believe in Christ *because* I believe in the miracles recorded in the Gospels, I believe in the miracles *because* I believe in Christ. So too I believe that Christ is the same yesterday, to-day, and for ever, not because I have seen so much evidence of His Healing Grace; but I look for His Grace to be manifested in healing the sick because I believe that He is the same for evermore.

The case for Divine Healing does not depend upon the evidence we can bring forward, but upon the promises of God; and it is a poor sort of faith which refuses to believe till it has seen signs and wonders, or has received records of them, signed and attested by doctors. We are taught that signs *follow* belief, not that they will be given to compel the sceptical to believe that the promises of God are really true.

The cases I mention, therefore, may be regarded merely as illustrations, and if they were all omitted it would make no difference to the book, as they are used to illustrate, not to prove my case.

Those who accept the teaching will have no difficulty in accepting the illustrations, and will probably be encouraged by them. Those who would only believe them if certified by a doctor, would hardly be likely to accept the teaching of the book.

" If they hear not Moses and the prophets, neither will they be persuaded though one rose from the dead."

E. HOWARD COBB.

THE HOME OF DIVINE HEALING,
    CROWHURST,
        March, 1933.

CONTENTS

CHRIST HEALING

CHAPTER I

CLEARING THE GROUND

FIRST of all, let me state our case, which is simply this:

Christ healed all the sick who came to Him in faith, or who were brought to Him by the faith of their friends.

He must therefore be as willing, and as able, to heal all the sick to-day; or else He is not "the same yesterday, to-day, and for ever."

This is the simple Gospel teaching, and has nothing to do with the various modern cults of healing, such as "Christian Science"; healing through Spiritism; or by the exercise of the human will.

"Christian Science" can certainly teach us a good deal with regard to the place sickness takes in life, but it is based on a fantastic theory of the unreality of evil, instead of upon the solid foundation of the Atonement. Spiritism seeks the aid of the spirits of departed doctors, instead of the Spirit of the Great Physician: while healing by the power of one's own will is far more likely, if successful, to make one self-conscious than God-conscious.

Divine Healing is simply the Healing of Christ through His Church, as instituted by our Lord Himself, as carried on by the Apostles, and for several centuries more by the ministry of the Church.

The Ministry of Healing, though never lost entirely, lapsed from general use when the Church grew too prosperous and worldly, and lost faith in her own power, or rather in her privilege of being used as the channel of Divine power.

That this power is still available for the healing of suffering humanity is abundantly proved by the many cases of healing, through faith in the Name of Jesus, which are in evidence on every side.

My purpose is to examine the foundations for this belief, and to show how this healing may be realized in the life of every follower of our Lord.

Before building a house it is necessary to clear the site, and then lay foundations ; so I propose that, before going any farther, we should proceed to clear the ground of the many objections which are constantly being put forward.

I

The first objection likely to occur to the mind of any one who has always regarded miraculous healing as belonging only to the Apostolic age, is that of possibility. How can an organic disease, or even a functional disorder, be healed without " doing anything," without taking medicine, or resorting to the skill of the surgeon? How can the Laying on of Hands, or the Anointing with Oil, or simple prayer, bring about a radical change in the material body? To doubt the possibility is surely to leave God out of the question.

I do not suggest for one moment that I have in my hands any power to heal, or that oil, even when blessed by a Bishop, has any therapeutic value; but I do believe, in fact I know from experience, that God can use my hands, or the consecrated oil, as the channel of His Grace, to cast out disease, and to bring new life and strength to an infirm body.

Nor is it unscientific, as many people might imagine. The body is constantly changing, new cells are replacing the old. Every muscular effort uses up cells which are continually being replaced. Whenever damage is done, "Nature" sets to work to repair it. If you cut your finger, the pain telegraphs the fact to the brain, through the elaborate system of nerves with which the body is equipped, and that part of the subconscious mind which deals with such matters, causes a larger number of the red corpuscles in the blood to hasten to the scene of the accident to build up the tissues which have been destroyed.

If you get some foreign substance into your finger, the action is similar, only this time it is the white corpuscles which are sent to surround the substance, and so prevent it from causing harm.

The mind thus controls the body. We call it

" Nature," but that is only a way of describing the working of God's plan.

The power of the mind over the body is probably unlimited. An experiment once made in this direction is instructive. A woman hypnotized, and then touched on the hand with an ordinary fountain pen, was told that it was a piece of hot iron. The touch not only caused her to show signs of pain, but actually raised a blister. Her hand was touched a second time, and she was told that the iron was hotter. The result was another blister, which took longer to clear away than the first.

The power of the mind over the body is universally recognized, and regarded by the medical profession as a most potent means of healing. If we go one step further and realize—as we must do if we believe the plain teaching of the Scriptures—the power of the *Spirit* over the mind, we see how Divine Healing is brought about by the Spirit of God using the natural machinery for healing, with which He has equipped the human body. If the Spirit of God can control the mind, He can, through the mind, control the body also ; and the faith which accepts Him as the controller of the mind, is the faith which accepts Him as the healer of the body.

Once again, let us remember that our bodies are continually changing as the cells are being continually rebuilt. To what pattern are they being rebuilt ? To that which is impressed upon the mind. If the mind is continually dwelling upon the imperfection in the body, we can hardly expect the cells to be rebuilt to any other pattern. If, on the other hand, the mind is continually dwelling on the thought of perfection, that perfection will become manifest in the body, and the cells will be rebuilt according to the perfect plan of God, instead of being mere reproductions of the imperfect cells they replace. Here again we see the work of the Holy Spirit, as we realize that faith in the promises of God enables Him to fill the mind with that image of perfection, which will bring healing, as the perfection becomes manifested in the body.

The mending of a broken bone is one of the best examples of what we call natural healing; and "Nature" is but another way of expressing the power behind it; which is God. We take the mending of the bone so much as a matter of course, that we fail to regard it as anything extraordinary, though it is, in reality, an amazing proof of the recuperative power with which the human body is endowed; and if that is so universally possible, why should we regard the healing of other parts, or organs, of the body as impossible: for we must remember that the most skilful doctor can only set the broken bone; it is the natural power, the *vis medicatrix naturæ* which mends it.

While accepting the general principle, one may perhaps be excused for feeling some uncertainty as to how far we may expect the Holy Spirit of God to use this recuperative power. There are many who are prepared to believe in Divine Healing for nervous or even functional disorders but refuse to believe that organic diseases can be so cured. The test case is generally cancer, commonly regarded as the most dreadful of all diseases, and the most hopelessly incurable. Of course the doctors do not really regard it as incurable, or they would not spend so much effort in the search for the cure. When they call it incurable they simply mean that, up to the present, no certain remedy for it has been discovered. The fact that Science has not yet discovered the remedy, is no proof that the Almighty Creator of the universe is unable to mend, or to remake, that which He has created. Scientists to-day are very unwilling to declare things impossible. Their conclusions must be based on ascertained facts, otherwise they would not be scientific. Facts can prove what is possible ; but he would be a bold man who would, in these days, claim that ascertained facts could prove the impossibility of healing any disease ; because there is always the chance that some hitherto unknown fact may be discovered which would overthrow his conclusions. As a matter of fact it has been proved beyond all question that cancer cases have been healed by the healing Grace of God. I know of several such cases ; where medical testimony has been given both before and after. Sometimes when such cases are healed, an attempt is made to question the correctness of the diagnosis ; though I can never understand why any doctor should prefer to admit that he had been mistaken, rather than recognize a manifestation of the power of God.

After all, it does not really matter whether we think it possible or not ; facts speak for themselves ; and facts all go to prove that the Sacramental use

of consecrated oil, and the laying on of hands, are
both channels of the healing Grace of God; and
there is no reason to doubt that the Grace so given,
works through the natural recuperative power, with
which God Himself has endowed the human body.

II

The next objection usually put forward is the
question of God's will. Perhaps it is not His will
that I should be healed; this sickness may be the
cross I have to carry.

This question is best answered by another. What
is the Scriptural authority for such a supposition?
Can you tell me of any case of sickness which Christ
refused to heal; or of any instance of His telling
the sufferer that it was for his good that he should
continue to bear his sickness patiently? Can you
find any text suggesting that He ever uttered any
Beatitude for the sick? We read frequently in the
Gospels that He healed *all* the sick who came to
Him in faith, or were brought to Him by the faith
of their friends.

If He was willing to heal all the sick who came
to Him during his life on earth, He must be equally
willing to-day—or else He has changed. It is sometimes argued that circumstances have changed, and
that He was performing miracles of healing to prove
that His Ministry was of God; and that such proof
is not necessary now. That idea originated at the
time of the Reformation, when, in order to discredit
the claim for miracles wrought by the reliques of

the Saints, it was declared that the age of miracles was over, and no such manifestations were to be expected. To-day the idea itself is proved to be false by the many miracles of healing, which are in evidence for all who will take the trouble to inquire. Let any doubter read Mr. Hickson's account of his Healing Missions, in his book *Heal the Sick*, and his doubts will soon be dispelled.

If Christ did use healing for the purpose suggested, it was only a secondary one ; the primary purpose obviously being to manifest the Love of God, and to prove that the Kingdom of God was nigh.

No matter how circumstances may change, Christ cannot change, therefore He is as willing to heal the sick to-day as He was then, or He is not " the same yesterday, to-day, and for ever." Further reasons for this assertion will be given when we come to the laying of the foundations ; now we are only trying to clear the site.

The only case that can be brought forward which suggests the possibility that God is unwilling to heal under certain circumstances, is that of St. Paul's thorn in the flesh ; and as I have never yet addressed a meeting on the subject of healing without this question being raised, it is clearly one that demands attention.

No one knows with any certainty what the " thorn " was, and many commentators have regarded it as a moral difficulty. I doubt if there is much ground for such an interpretation, which one might almost suspect to be an endeavour to simplify the problem. The more general interpretation is that it was a physical infirmity, and as such I prefer to regard it.

First of all, let us note that St. Paul does not say that it was sent by God, but that it was " a messenger of Satan " which was allowed to trouble him in order to save him from the spiritual pride, which might easily have taken possession of him, as the result of the vision which had been given to him. Thrice he prayed that it might be taken away, and each time the answer from God was the same : " My Grace is sufficient for thee." Now, is the Grace of God given to us to enable us to put up with an evil thing, or to save us from its power ? Surely for the latter purpose. Should we not then regard this " thorn " as an ever-present threat, sufficient to keep him from spiritual pride, but unable to hinder him in his work, as long as he remembered his absolute dependence upon God, and continually sought the protection of His Grace ? As an example of what I mean, take the case of a man threatened with rheumatism, who keeps well as long as he takes his daily dose of salts ; but experiences twinges of pain as soon as he neglects the protective remedy. It is an unworthy simile, but it explains my meaning : the threat was ever present, but the Grace of God was sufficient to protect him from its power.

We are told that this continued threat was for the purpose of protecting St. Paul from the temptation to spiritual pride ; therefore the need of such a warning ought to pass away with growth in spiritual grace.

Have we any proof that the " thorn " continued
to the end of St. Paul's life ? It is only in the
Second Epistle to the Corinthians that he records
his desire to be delivered from it ; and he lived some
years after the writing of that Epistle. He refers
to it again in his letter to the Galatians (Gal. iv. 13),
where he writes of it as having been in evidence
during his first visit, but not when he went to them
the second time. This is not observable in the
English translation, but it is made very clear in the
Greek, by the use of the aorist tense. Had the
" thorn " been still threatening him, at the time of
his second visit, he would have used the imperfect
tense. The use of the aorist proves that it had
ceased to be ; as the Greek tenses are very exact ;
and the aorist could not have been used of a thing
still in existence.

St. Paul is the outstanding witness of Divine
Healing. Think for a moment of the sufferings he
endured ; " Five times received I forty stripes save
one, thrice was I beaten with rods." Eight scourg-
ings, any one of which might have proved fatal ;
and yet he was able to carry on his work ! At
Lystra he was stoned, and cast out of the city as
dead, which is sufficient proof of the severity of the
stoning ; yet he rose up and proceeded on his way,
being at work again on the following day. In the
first chapter of the Second Epistle to the Corinthians
he writes of an illness which had attacked him in
Asia, from which he had been healed by prayer :
and again on the island of Malta he was healed of
the serpent's bite. You will see, therefore, that I

am glad when the question regarding St. Paul is put forward, because his life does far more to prove our case than to furnish an exception.

Some will undoubtedly ask, "Have we not to be made perfect through suffering; may not sickness be a part of life's discipline?"

If that is really so, we ought to be very careful how we take steps to seek healing; lest we be found to be trying to act against the will of God. We often find people trying to console themselves with this thought, when every remedy has failed to bring relief; but I have never found any one refusing to seek healing for fear of opposing the will of God. Even when the long-continued suffering has been accepted as God's will, that never seems to stand in the way of using every available means which might effect a cure. I remember a patient once telling me that she was convinced that the pain from which she was suffering was the cross she had to bear. Her conviction seemed to weaken when I pointed out to her that, if that were so, she had no right to go on taking drugs to lessen the pain.

It is certainly true that we must be made perfect through suffering; but it is equally certain that the suffering which will help towards perfection must be *voluntary*; and sickness can hardly be counted as that. If we are to share in the sufferings of our Lord, it must be in self-denial, and willingness to suffer persecution for His sake. We cannot share His sufferings in bearing sickness, for there is no record that He was ever touched by disease; nor indeed could He be touched by it, seeing that it is essentially evil. Truly He bore the burden of sickness upon the Cross; but though He endured the pain, the fever, and the thirst, which are the result of sickness; in His case they were not caused by disease, but by the cruelty of His enemies.

No one will deny that many have found much consolation, and strength to bear their sufferings patiently, by believing that, in so doing, they were submitting to the will of God. I have no doubt that we could all quote instances of real spiritual growth as the result of such patience; but nothing will make me believe that our Heavenly Father sends sickness, when we can never believe that any earthly father, worthy of the name, would do such a thing. I am, however, quite ready to believe that, when sickness comes, God uses the opportunity to teach some spiritual lesson, and that healing may be delayed till the lesson has been learned. The very fact that a thing is educational implies that it is temporary, to be put aside when the lesson has been learned, so that, however great the Grace given during the time of learning, the greater Grace would be manifested in the removal of the discipline at the end of the course of instruction. "Shall we continue in sin that Grace may abound?" Most certainly not: the greater Grace is experienced in the delivery from sin. Does not the same apply to sickness? The greater Grace is manifested in the healing.

III

Another objection will assuredly be, the number of those who remain unhealed, in spite of earnest prayers and apparently true faith. It is a very real objection which I have no intention of avoiding; but it is one which I cannot deal with fully here, as other questions, which must be considered later, are involved in it. We shall have to consider the real meaning of the prayer of faith; the motive underlying the desire for healing; and the possible hindrances which may be caused by sin, or a wrong attitude towards God. There is, however, one side of the question which we shall do well to face as soon as possible, and that is the possibility that we ourselves may be hindering the healing of our friends. We read of the occasion when Christ Himself could do no mighty works because of the unbelief of the people. Is not the unbelief of the Church the greatest hindrance to healing that we have to face to-day? When we speak of the Church we mean not only the clergy, but the laity as well. Let us each face the question honestly; Is the faith of the Church strengthened or weakened by my membership? It is quite possible that our own want of faith is contributing to the barrier of unbelief, which is hindering the healing we are so anxious to see, and which we are requiring as the proof to convince us. Christ does not promise to give us proofs to *make* us believe, but signs that will *follow* belief.

I have myself known of several cases where the

unbelief of friends and relatives was an undoubted hindrance to healing, not only setting up a barrier against the healing Grace of God, but also weakening the faith of the patient.

I have even known sick people refuse to have their names mentioned in church, with a request for the prayers of the congregation ; not because they did not believe in the power of prayer, but because they knew that such a request is so often regarded as a sign that there is little hope of recovery ; thus arousing in the minds of the neighbours a feeling of anxiety, which is really the barrier of unbelief. To such a pass have we come, that the Church, which should be the channel of the Healing Grace, has become an instrument in raising a barrier of unbelief, which hinders the manifestation of that Grace.

IV

There are still two other difficulties met with from time to time, which are best considered here.

One is the question of death. If everybody is to be healed, how are we going to die ? The God, Who is the Author of Life, does not need disease to destroy life. When He is ready He can quietly withdraw the life He gave, and call His child home. The leaves fall from the trees when their purpose is accomplished ; they do not need to be diseased, or stripped off by a storm. The natural death should be a quiet passing to the Spirit World, when God withdraws the spirit from the body ; rather than the body becoming, by disease, unfit for the spirit to dwell in any longer. Such passings are not infrequent, and one cannot but believe that they are far more in accordance with the will of the Loving Father, than the passings which are brought about by some agonizing disease.

The other difficulty is the objection, often put forward, that believers in Divine Healing attach too much importance to the body. No one would ever suggest that the body is of equal importance with the soul; seeing that the soul is eternal, and the body but its temporary dwelling-place. The objection is based upon an entirely erroneous idea; and the true teaching of Divine Healing should have just the opposite effect. We believe that the body is the Temple of the Holy Spirit; so we are confident that it is the Will of God that the Temple should be undefiled by sickness, as well as unstained by sin. Full and complete acceptance of Christ's teaching would take away all fear of sickness, and the constant apprehension that every little ache or pain might be the threat of some calamity. There should be no need for continual anxiety about health, with all its attendant preparations to ward off disease. Think of all the people to-day who are surrounded by their remedies, their lotions, and their salves; doses to prevent colds, draughts to induce sleep, tabloids to relieve pain; with their medical adviser, their nerve specialist, their throat specialist, their dentist, their optician, and their masseuse; their diet sheet, and special rules for taking nourishment and exercises. Surely they are the people who are paying the vast amount of attention to the body, and living in constant fear of something going wrong. And yet many so encumbered—and their name is Legion—do actually accuse the believer in Divine Healing of making the body too important, because he is confident that our Heavenly Father is so careful for that which He has created and which has been sanctified by our Lord's use of it, that he can safely commit it to His keeping, without all the anxious cares and preparations deemed necessary by those who hold no such belief.

I hope that we can now put the negatives on one side, and start to consider positives ; that, having cleared the site, we can proceed to lay the foundations, by examining the Scriptural Truths upon which faith in Divine Healing is built up. I do not flatter myself that I have cleared away all the doubts, but I do hope that I have been allowed to show that the subject is worth further consideration ; and not such a fantastic idea as many still seem to think.

CHAPTER II

FOUNDATIONS

HAVING cleared the site as far as we can, we must now lay the foundations of our building.

I

The first one is to be found in the Book of Exodus, chap. xv., verses 22–26. After the crossing of the Red Sea, Moses had led the people of Israel through the wilderness for three days without water. Their physical condition must have been reduced to the lowest possible limit ; water they must have, or they must perish ; and the water, when they found it, was bitter and undrinkable. Return was impossible ; nothing but the intervention of God could save them. Moses was shown the way to make the water fit for use. Again the people were saved by the Grace of God. He had shown them that they were absolutely dependent upon Him, not only for their deliverance from oppression, but for their very existence. Then we read that God made a Statute, and an Ordinance, with His people.

A Statute was a Law of the Kingdom, and an Ordinance a Law of the Church ; therefore this was a Law both civil and ecclesiastical. The Law He gave them was the Law of Health, dependent upon obedience. If they would keep His Commandments, and obey His Word, they would be exempt from the diseases which had fallen upon the Egyptians ; but if they refused to obey, the diseases would fall upon them. God declared Himself to be the Guardian of His people's health : " I am the Lord that healeth thee." Health was thus established as the Law of God's people, and sickness declared to be the result of disobedience—a thing essentially evil.

The Will of God for His people is health of body, as well as purity of soul ; and God the Father is Himself the Healer. Here then the fact is established, that sickness and disease are essentially evil in origin and nature.

Science may trace the germs which cause disease, they may classify and discover the means of destroying them, but the fact that an illness may be traced to the introduction of germs into the system does nothing to prove that the illness is not evil in itself, or produced by evil. Did not Christ Himself attribute some sicknesses to the direct action of evil ? He rebuked the fever in St. Peter's wife's mother ; and He spoke of the woman, bowed down by infirmity for eighteen years, as one whom Satan had bound.

I remember the case of a young boy who had been ill for about a fortnight, with a sickness that the doctors diagnosed as gastric influenza. I had prayed over him, and laid hands upon him, and he had recovered to a certain extent; but did not completely throw off the trouble. His temperature remained high, and medicine for the purpose of reducing it was administered for four days without having the slightest effect. While praying with him on the following day, I felt moved to lay hands on him again, for the express purpose of driving out a power of evil. The same evening his temperature was a degree lower; and by the next morning it was normal.

A similar case was that of a lady, who was making but slow progress after an operation. Again it was given to me to feel that she was being hindered by a power of evil; and inasmuch as progress towards recovery became steady and pronounced, after laying hands on her for the purpose of driving out evil, I had no doubt that that was the real cause of the trouble.

There are many to-day who refuse to believe in a spiritual power of evil working to destroy the souls and the bodies of men; but Christ, who knew more of the unseen world than the wisdom of man can ever discover, constantly spoke, and acted, in a way that must have convinced His followers that the powers of evil are a terrible reality. Was it not for the purpose of delivering man from that power that He gave Himself to die upon the Cross? There was no doubt about it in the mind of St. Paul when he wrote: "For we wrestle not against flesh and blood, but against principalities, against powers, against the rulers of the darkness of this world, against spiritual wickedness in high places."

No one who has had any experience of Divine Healing can doubt it ; and I have come across a number of doctors who are convinced that many cases of insanity are really cases of possession, as well as many, if not all, cases of epilepsy. Personally I have never felt the power of evil more acutely than in the presence of an epileptic during a bad seizure. After all, if man is capable of being indwelt by the Holy Spirit of God, is it unlikely that he can be exposed to the attacks of evil spirits, if his heart is not fully surrendered to God ?

II

For our next foundation-stone we turn to Isaiah, chap. liii., verse 4 : " Surely he hath borne our griefs, and carried our sorrows."

If we turn to St. Matthew viii. 17, we read, " that it might be fulfilled which was spoken by Isaiah the prophet, saying, Himself took our infirmities and bare our sicknesses." Here we come nearer to the correct translation, as Hebrew scholars are agreed that the rendering of the words should be " sicknesses " and " pains " ; not " griefs " and " sorrows." We can go farther than this, and we find that the Hebrew verb translated " bare," is the very same verb used in the last verse of the chapter for the bearing of sins. The full meaning of the word is to " bear as a substitute." If Christ bore our sicknesses in the same way as He bore our sins—and the use of the same verb proves that He did—it can only mean that He bore them as our substitute. Thus the bearing of our sicknesses is clearly shown to be a part of the work of the Atonement. Can we doubt any longer that it is God's will to heal *all* sickness ? When we come to Him to seek healing we are not coming to ask Him to do something fresh for us ; but that it may be granted to us to share in that which has already been accomplished.

We see, then, God as the loving Father who gave His Only Son to save His people, not only from their sins, but also from the awful results of sin— the sicknesses which defile the bodies He has created to be Temples for His own indwelling.

Christ Jesus, our Lord, God the Son, is the Saviour of our souls and bodies. By His death upon the Cross He has broken down the barrier raised by sin, which separates us from the Father's Love ; and has become the Channel through which that Love can flow freely to us.

III

Our third foundation-stone is to be found in the Epistle of St. Paul to the Romans, chap. viii., verse 11 : " But if the Spirit of Him that raised up Jesus from the dead dwelleth in you, He that raised up Christ Jesus from the dead shall quicken also your mortal bodies through His Spirit that dwelleth in you." The key to this verse lies in the words " mortal bodies." The Greek word so translated

cannot mean dead bodies, it is always used to mean
living bodies, subject to mortality certainly, but
bodies which are alive. So we see that this verse
does not refer to the final quickening of the dead,
but to the power of the Holy Spirit to work in us
the healing Grace of God. If the Holy Spirit could
bring new life to the dead body of Jesus, surely He
can give renewed life to our living bodies.

Thus we see God the Father as the Fount of
Healing Love ; God the Son as our Healer, the
Administrator of the Father's Healing Grace ; and
God the Holy Spirit as the Power of God manifesting
Healing in our bodies, and filling us with the
abundant Life of Christ.

Here we have a foundation against which all the
winds of scepticism and floods of unbelief can hurl
themselves in vain. Can you imagine yourself
standing in the presence of Christ, and saying to
Him, " Lord Jesus, I believe that on Thy Cross
Thou didst bear the sicknesses of all mankind, but
I do not believe that Thou wast able to bear mine ? "
It is absolutely unthinkable.

IV

There are some, we know, who at times are filled
with doubts as to whether they can share in the
forgiveness of sins ; who think that they have
committed sins which cannot be pardoned ; but
this is only the case when the mind is too clouded
to be able to accept the clear promises of God ; or

when egotism has reached such a pitch that they think they have been capable of committing a sin so heinous, that it is beyond the power of the cleansing Blood of the Redeemer to wash it away.

We know that the only unforgivable sin is the sin against the Holy Ghost, which means not some particular sin, so terrible that God is unwilling, or unable, to forgive in answer to true penitence; but a state of sin which denies the power of the Holy Spirit; and unforgivable because unrepented. Forgiveness requires penitential confession, and confession depends upon sorrow for the sin committed. There can be no sorrow till the heart is convicted of sin. It is the Holy Spirit who alone can convict; so that the denial of the Holy Spirit renders penitence, and therefore forgiveness, impossible.

Seeing, then, that Christ has made the healing of our bodies, as well as the forgiveness of our sins, a part of His atoning Sacrifice, it follows that no sickness can be incurable, unless there be refusal to accept the working of the Holy Spirit. Not, of course, that we need the power of the Spirit to make us aware of our sickness; but that it is He alone Who can manifest the Healing Grace in our lives.

Building on our foundations we find that Christ healed all the sick who came to Him in faith, that He made it abundantly clear that sickness had no place in His Kingdom; "He went about doing good," and "healing all who were oppressed of the devil." We find that He commissioned His Church to carry on His work ; He promised that where there was faith, the laying on of hands would bring healing : " The works that I do shall ye do also, and greater works than these shall ye do." We read in the Acts of the Apostles that the Ministry of Healing was carried on ; and we are told that when the sick folk were brought to Jerusalem from towns and villages round about, they were healed *every one*—and still there are many who doubt !

We can see now that, when we come to seek healing from God, we are not to ask Him to show His compassion by taking pity on our sad condition. We are to assure Him that we do believe that it is His will to heal us, and to ask to be allowed to share in the full glory of Redemption.

We come, not to ask Him to send forth more Grace to us, but to enable us to receive the Grace which is always pouring forth from Him.

We come, not to ask, but to receive ; and what we need to learn is, *how* to receive. This will be the subject of the next chapters : first the means of reception appointed by our Lord, and then the necessary condition of heart and mind.

CHAPTER III

THE SACRAMENTS OF HEALING

NOW fully convinced, I hope, not by my words, but by the words of the Bible, we can approach our Lord with full assurance that He is willing to deliver us from all sickness, and to fill us with His abundant Life. The question now is, How shall we seek to share in this glorious gift? Is prayer alone sufficient, or must we seek sacramental means, such as the Laying on of Hands, or Anointing with Oil?

There is abundant evidence that many have been healed through prayer alone, some through their own prayers, and others through the prayers of their friends. I call to mind particularly the case of one suffering from appendicitis who went into hospital for an operation, but was so completely healed through the prayers of a circle of believers, that the operation was unnecessary. Of the individual cases of healing recorded in the Gospels, there are twice as many healed through faith of their friends as those who came in their own faith. Nor is this strange, because it is easier for friends to think of the sufferer as he ought to be, than for the sufferer himself to do so. There are many illnesses which are accompanied by so much pain that it is almost impossible for the average man to prevent his mind from being obsessed with the thought of it ; and many where any effort of prayer is practically impossible.

The chief difficulty in relying on prayer alone is that of knowing when to change prayer to thanksgiving. The difficulty may not be apparent at first sight, as many would say that the time for thanksgiving is obviously the time when the healing is granted ; but here we are considering the prayer of faith, and faith does not wait for evidence ; it believes in promises.

When there is personal experience of the Living Christ, and the sick person is able to remain in prayer till a definite assurance is received, thanksgiving would naturally begin at once, irrespective of symptoms. There is the case of Mrs. Bainbridge, who wrote several very helpful books on healing, which are, unfortunately, I believe, out of print. In one of these she records how she herself was becoming deaf. She prayed for healing, waiting upon God till she received the assurance that her prayer was answered. She at once gave thanks, and continued to do so daily, though the deafness increased till she could only hear her husband when he shouted close to her ear. She believed the promise in spite of apparent failure ; and then, when her faith had been tested, her hearing was completely restored quite suddenly.

It is not every one who is so advanced in the
practice of prayer as to be able to receive an assurance strong enough to resist all temptation to give
up hope, if the desired result does not come quickly.
There is also the fact we have just noticed, that in
a time of sickness any concentration in prayer
becomes very difficult, if not quite impossible.
For most of us, therefore, it is advisable to seek
Ministration.

Apart from the fact that it is a Means of Grace—
which we will consider later—to seek it is an act of
faith. We have been praying for healing, and we
have reached the stage at which we believe that
Christ is holding out to us His gift of health ; then
by all means let us show our faith by coming to
receive the proffered Blessing. But are we ready
to do so ? The thought may come, " Supposing
that I do seek healing through the ministration of
the Church, and do not get better, shall I not be
worse off than before ? shall I not only remain
unhealed, but possibly lose my faith as well ? "

The test of readiness to receive is whether we are
prepared to give thanks without waiting to see the
result, and to go on giving thanks even if the healing
be delayed.

Nor is this as difficult as it may seem at first, if
we keep in mind the distinction between the sowing
of a seed and the growth of the seed after it has
been sown.

If you gave me the seed of some choice flower
planted in a pot, I should at once thank you for it ;
I should not wait till it had blossomed : your gift

would be an act complete in itself. The growth of that seed would then depend upon my keeping it in the right conditions of light, heat, and air.

If then you come to receive Christ's healing through the ministry of the Church, or through some one who has been endowed by God with the charismatic gift of healing, you undoubtedly receive Grace. Think of it as the sowing of a seed, an action complete in itself. Could you not then give thanks for that gift, and continue to give thanks, even though the growth might be slow ? If you believe that you have received a gift you cannot refrain from giving thanks.

As soon as the gift has been received, the form of our prayers must change. We must begin by giving thanks for the Grace we have received, and pray that nothing may hinder the growth thereof. To go on praying as if we had not received anything, because the result is not yet evident, would be an expression of faithlessness. We might compare it to the refusal to thank the giver of a cheque until we had passed it through the bank, in spite of the fact that it bears an absolutely trustworthy signature. In discussing this question with brother clergy this particular difficulty has often been put forward. " Suppose," one may say, " that I do minister to a sick person, who gets no better, how am I to explain the failure ? " I would reply with a counter question. " Would you withhold the Sacrament of Holy Communion from those whom you might consider unlikely to manifest the fruits thereof ? " Certainly not, because, in the first place, we have no right to judge such a question; and secondly, because we know that the Holy Sacrament is a Means of Grace. God gives the Grace in the Sacrament, not the faith of the recipient, though it will certainly not benefit him if he takes it without faith. The administration of the Sacrament is an action complete in itself, again like the sowing of a seed: the growth depends upon the soil in which it is sown, and the care bestowed upon it. Where this has been fully understood with regard to the Sacraments of healing, there can be no danger of losing faith, however long the healing may be delayed.

My advice to one about to seek healing through Ministration is to think only of the Grace to be received, and the Giver of it, and not to worry about what will happen afterwards. If fear as to the result is allowed to creep in it will weaken the faith in the Sacrament itself. If our minds are filled with the seriousness of the disease, and the possibility of its remaining unhealed, we are not likely to come with the faith which will be ours, if we keep our thoughts fixed on the gift we are about to receive, and, above all, on the Giver.

Many of my readers are familiar with the picture which appears on the cover of the *Healer Magazine*. It is that of a mother holding a sick child in her arms, and looking up at the face of Christ, who is stretching out His hand to heal. No one could look at the child in the mother's arms without feeling anxiety, it is so obviously very ill; but there

is no anxiety depicted in the face of the mother.
Her face is full of hope, because she is looking, not
at the child, but at the face of Jesus. When you
come to seek healing, think not of the man who is
about to minister to you, but realize that you are
coming to the Christ, who is stretching out His
hand to heal you : look not at your present troubles,
which may easily stimulate fear for the future, but
at the face of Him Who bore your own particular
sickness upon His Cross, and is longing to release
you from it. Then, because you know that you
have received His gift of Grace, give thanks without
delay ; and continue to give thanks whether the
healing be delayed, or comes immediately.

It is quite probable that, if the healing is long
delayed, a feeling of unreality may arise in the
mind. One may be tempted to think that it savours
of hypocrisy to go on giving thanks, when no
improvement is perceptible. If this temptation
comes, it is only necessary to analyse our meaning,
and to realize that we have received a gift of Grace,
and we shall see that to cease to give thanks would
be a confession that we do not trust the promise
of our Lord. A similar feeling is sometimes experienced with regard to the making of affirmations.
Here it is necessary to be on our guard. Never go
on making an affirmation which you feel instinctively
to be untrue. You cannot bluff your subconscious
mind ; nor can you force it to believe that which
it instinctively rejects. To continue the affirmation
under such conditions is merely to strengthen the

resistance. Analyse your affirmation, till you have assured yourself that, although there may be no evidence of its reality, it is nevertheless based upon the fundamental truths of the revealed Word of God : you can then continue to make it with the certainty that by so doing you are establishing that truth in your heart.

I am often asked what is the difference, if any, between the Laying on of Hands, and Anointing with Oil. There is certainly no justification for supposing that either is more likely to bring healing than the other, for both are but the channel of Grace. Healing comes from Christ, and from Him alone. Even in the case of a charismatic gift of healing, it can only mean that the one so endowed is a more open channel than those who have not the gift.

Both forms of Ministration are Scriptural, and, I would maintain, instituted by Christ Himself. In the account of the mission of the Twelve given by St. Mark (vi. 13) we read that " they anointed with oil many that were sick, and healed them." Nor can I believe that they would have done so without instruction, especially when we read of the detailed instructions which Christ gave them concerning their conduct and equipment. The Laying on of Hands was the direct command of our Lord a short time before His Ascension (St. Mark xvi.).

Present-day use of these means gives no indication of any distinction, as there are just as remarkable cases of healing following the one as the other. In practice, however, there is this difference, that Anointing is generally used once only in the same period of sickness ; whereas the Laying on of Hands is repeated frequently. The idea that Unction may be used three times, but not more than three, is based on the misreading of St. Paul's thrice-repeated request to be delivered from his thorn. It seems to suggest that we might expect God to change His mind after one, or even two refusals, but not after three. When we know that the deliverance from sickness is part of the work of the Atonement we realize the error of such an idea. Again, the scope of Anointing seems to be wider than that of the Laying on of Hands. We remember that not only the sick, but kings, prophets, and priests were anointed, which seems to imply that the Oil of Anointing was the seal of God's acceptance of a life consecrated to His service. Personally I like to emphasize that aspect in anointing the sick. There can be no higher thought than that of re-dedicating one's life to God, with the assurance that He, willing to use us in His service, may be depended upon to make, and keep, us usable. Thus the Oil is the seal of His acceptance, as well as the channel of healing Grace. When Anointing is sought in this way it would obviously be unseemly to repeat it, unless some subsequent attack of sickness renders us again unfit for use. The Laying on of Hands seems to be less comprehensive, and can be used frequently as the means of seeking the continuance of the Grace already received, or, if you like to put it so, for the watering of the seed already sown : although of course it can be, and is frequently used as the only channel through which the healing Grace is expected. Whatever we do we must avoid any idea of trying again, as though the first attempt had been unsuccessful. The Laying on of Hands, when repeated, or when used after Anointing, must always be for the *continuance* of the Grace already received.

We must admit that Anointing may be a greater help to the faith of some, inasmuch as it is more definitely sacramental, and is generally accompanied by a fuller Service of prayer : also in cases of extreme danger it may help us to feel that we have done all that we, on our part, could do ; though this is really a concession to human weakness There is perhaps another advantage attached to the use of Anointing, and that is that there is less danger of considering any personal element. I have heard people express a preference for receiving the Laying on of Hands from Mr. X. rather than from Mr. Y. or Mr. Z. because " he does me more good." This must be altogether wrong, as it is Christ alone Who is the Healer. The virtue in Anointing, on the other hand, is less liable to be associated with the man who administers it ; just as with Holy Communion, though we may like the manner of Mr. X. in conducting the Service better than that of Mr. Y. we do not expect to receive greater Grace at his hands.

Whenever possible I prefer to leave the choice of means to the patient, urging that guidance should

be sought in prayer; but if no guidance seems
to be given, that the patient should choose that
which he feels would be the greater help to his
faith.

In any case, we must remember that both are, in
one sense, acts of faith, and should be *asked for*.
I may do my best to explain the meaning, but it is
not for me, or for any other priest, to urge a sick
person to " try " either. St. James (v. 14) expressly
states that the sick man must *send* for the Elders
of the Church—that is the test of his faith.

There are some who would tempt us to believe
that the value of both these Means of Grace is
merely psychological. To do so is not only to deny
the teaching of Scripture, but also to ignore facts.
Six times I have myself seen the flow of blood from
a severed artery stopped instantaneously by the
Grace given through the Laying on of Hands with
prayer, when no medical means whatever were used.
It is hard to believe that this could be accomplished
by suggestion ; and certainly no human power
could do it. To me, at any rate, it was convincing
proof of the presence of the Healing Christ, making
use of human hands as the channel of His Grace.
I have also known an abscess disappear in a night
without coming to a head and breaking, which is
hardly likely to happen through the power of suggestion. There is, however, nothing to be gained
by emphasizing the point. Those who are determined to continue in disbelief will not be convinced
by argument, or by fact ; and I expect that those

who have read so far have done so because they
were already convinced.

You may possibly have come across the objection
that the Greek word for " anointing " used by St.
James always means " to massage," or " to smear,"
and therefore the anointing was used medically
rather than sacramentally. Before we accept that
argument we must consider the fact that the same
word is used in Exodus xl. 17 (Septuagint version)
for the anointing of the sons of Aaron ; while in
the previous verse a different word is used for the
anointing of Aaron himself, though it is distinctly
stated that the sons were to be anointed *in the same
manner* as the father. The word used for the
anointing of Aaron is the word that is used for the
anointing of Jesus with the Holy Ghost. This
word, meaning " to touch with oil," is used for the
Son of God, and for God's High Priest ; but the
lesser word is used for the anointing of the House
of Aaron, and the House, or Church, of Christ.
The Scripture distinctly says that the manner is to
be the same, that is to say, touching, not rubbing,
with the oil, and after all, the Anointing is but
the outward and visible sign of the inward and
spiritual Grace. St. James states that it is the
prayer of faith which shall save the sick, and
whether we seek healing through Anointing, or the
Laying on of Hands, the prayer of faith is the all-
important thing. We must return then to this
thought, and consider it in a fresh chapter ; but
before doing so I would point out that there is still

another Sacrament of Healing, and that is the greatest of all, the Sacrament of the Body and Blood of Jesus Christ.

Some time ago a lady, who was coming from one of the far-distant parts of the Empire to undergo an operation at the hands of a famous surgeon, was meditating on the Communion Service, when she was struck by the words of the Administration, " Preserve thy *body* and soul. . . ." She had not realized before that the Grace of Communion is for the body as well as for the soul ; but having done so, she partook of the Sacrament in that belief, and found healing thereby—the operation was not necessary. The Sacrament of Holy Communion can be viewed from different aspects. It is our Eucharist, or Service of Thanksgiving ; in it we show forth the Lord's Death until He comes again ; it is our pleading before God the Eternal Sacrifice of the Cross : but when we partake of the Bread and Wine, which He has commanded to be received, we partake of the Body and Blood of Christ, " which are verily and indeed taken and received by the faithful in that Sacrament." The Body and Blood of Jesus imparted to us, that our bodies may be made more fit Temples for the indwelling of His Spirit ; " that our bodies may be made clean by His Body, and our souls washed through His most precious Blood, that we may evermore dwell in Him, and He in us." How could it fail to be a healing Sacrament to those who believe the full Gospel of Salvation for spirit, soul, and body ? Why should we expect to receive cleansing for the soul, and ignore the cleansing, or healing, of our bodies, when our Lord gave Himself to die upon the Cross to effect both ? The Temple for His indwelling should no more be defiled by disease than by sin, and Christ has made provision for the healing as well as for the cleansing.

CHAPTER IV

THE PRAYER OF FAITH

AS we have already noted, St. James clearly states that it is the prayer of *faith* which will save the sick. He gives no such assurance to the prayer of hope, or of despair.

Speaking of prayer he says (chap. i. verse 6, Revised Version): "But let him ask in faith, nothing doubting: for he that doubteth is like the surge of the sea driven by the wind and tossed. For let not that man think that he shall receive anything of the Lord."

Faith must be based upon knowledge.

First of all, we know that God is *able* to heal. There is abundant evidence of that.

We know, too, that healing is God's will, because we know that Christ bore the burden of our sicknesses upon the Cross; and therefore our prayer must not be weakened by the qualification, "if it be Thy will." We should never dream of qualifying our prayer for the forgiveness of sin in that way, so why should we qualify the prayer to be made partakers of that blessing which was procured for us at the same time, and in the same way ?

Faith, however, means something more than knowledge of doctrine, no matter how sure that knowledge may be.

Faith means knowledge of God Himself. It is not sufficient to know *about* Him, we must *know* Him, or, what is probably easier for most of us to conceive, we must know Jesus Christ as our living Lord and Saviour.

Without the personal experience of Jesus Christ we cannot expect the promises of Scripture to outweigh the fears produced by the circumstances of life.

If you go to some medical specialist of great reputation, and he, after making a thorough examination, declares you to be suffering from an incurable disease, the verdict he gives has all the force of his personality behind it ; it introduces a fear thought into your subconscious mind, which will become a fixed idea, until it is overcome by an idea of greater power. The words of Scripture, the promises of our Lord, ought to have that greater power ; but how can they if they lack the force of personality which gave such power to the words of the specialist. It is not that we doubt their truth, but that they lack the power to overcome the fear thought ; and it is the thought that *is* dominant in the subconscious mind, not the thought that we should *like to be* dominant, which rules our life. You cannot overcome that fear by the power of the will ; in fact the harder you try, the stronger you make it ;

because every effort to overcome it is really an acknowledgment of its reality, and thus adds to its strength. If it were not there, there would be no need to fight it, so the effort to fight it proves you are afraid of it.

That fear can only be overcome by a stronger power, the power of the Truth. Now Truth has been defined as " agreement with reality," but the reality may not be the highest Truth, the Truth which is the eternal principle of right, the Truth as it is in Jesus.

It may be true, as a statement of fact, to say that a certain person is suffering from some disease, but the Truth, as it is in Jesus, is that the burden of that sickness has been borne by Him upon the Cross, and therefore it has no right to defile the body which is the Temple of the Holy Spirit.

Now if the Truth is to be the power which will make you free, it must have the force of personality of Jesus behind it, and it cannot have that force till we have personal experience of Jesus Christ.

Is this experience within the reach of all ? Most certainly, if we seek it in the appointed way. We are not going to find it through the emotions To seek it thus, only leads to alternations of exaltation and depression ; times when prayer and Sacraments seem to bring Him very near ; followed by times when He seems to have forsaken us entirely.

Not by the emotions, but through the Spirit, we shall find Christ. Hold fast to the truth that He is ever abiding in you, and that His Presence does not depend upon your feelings, but on His promise, and you are putting yourself in the position in which He can reveal Himself to you. Many are making desperate and sincere efforts to find Christ, but it is the very effort which hinders them from realizing their desire ; because effort means an attempt to find Him by means of the feelings, or emotions. We cannot find Him, but He can reveal Himself to us, because His Spirit is dwelling in us ; and it is through the Spirit that the revelation must come. As by adoration, praise, and expectant waiting we acknowledge our belief that His Spirit is within us, He will reveal Himself. It is " of God we are in Christ Jesus " ; that is to say, it is God the Holy Spirit, Who does, and Who alone can, give to us that instinctive realization of Him which can be even as fully convincing as sight itself.

We must believe His promise, and act as if we believe, then we can receive : and as fellowship becomes more real, His promises become more sure, because they have the force of His personality behind them. Jesus is very real to the little child. I remember a child, five years old, suffering from a severe attack of measles, covered with rash, asking Jesus to heal him. He had been taught to believe in Jesus as the Healer, so his prayer was the prayer of faith, and in two days' time the doctor pronounced him to be healed. Another case of childish faith is that of a boy of eight who was so sorely afflicted with asthma that the doctor feared that he would not live through another winter. I prayed over him, and laid hands on him in the Name of Jesus Christ. Two days later he was to return home, so I offered to lay hands on him again before he started on his journey, to claim a blessing for him. The answer brought to me was that he did not want to come ; he had got what he needed the first time, why should he come again ? He was quite right, he had received his blessing, and was healed of the asthma.

When our Lord tells us that we must be as little children, He does not mean in innocence only, but in simplicity of faith, and in readiness to learn of Him. You cannot teach a person who thinks he knows all you want to teach him, nor can God teach us His Truth, as long as we trust to our intellectual knowledge. When we are ready to admit that we know nothing, we are ready to be taught, and it will not be long before He starts to reveal Himself to us : at any rate that has been my own experience ; and my first satisfying realization of God did not come till I was ready to acknowledge that I knew nothing. I do not mean to suggest that we are not to use our intellects, and powers of reasoning, but that we must use them under the guidance of the Holy Spirit, and not merely by the light of worldly wisdom and human understanding.

The point I must emphasize above all others is the absolute necessity of personal experience of the living Christ. It is not merely a question of healing, but of life itself. Our Religion is of very little use without it ; it will fail to help us at the time of our greatest need. No matter how perfectly we keep the law, or fulfil the obligations of worship and service, it will break down as soon as any great strain is put upon it, if we have not learned to know Christ through the power of the indwelling Spirit. It is all very well to say that we know that we have received the Holy Spirit, because we have been baptized, and confirmed, and are regular Communicants. The question is not as to whether we have received the Gift—there is no doubt about that—but whether we are so instinctively conscious of His Presence that we are able to act, and do act, in the assurance that He is the source of our life and strength and peace. I have known many devoted followers of Christ, giving their lives to His service, who had not till late in life reached that state of realization. For over twenty years I preached the Gospel, fully convinced of the truth of it, but compelled to hope that those to whom I preached were finding more reality in it than I was myself. Since the day that I acknowledged that I knew nothing, and thus opened my heart to God, I have been able to preach it because I know from experience that it is true.

Realization comes to different people in different ways. Probably the most frequent way of its coming is in response to genuine surrender; when there is a real searching of the heart, and determination to regard nothing as one's own; to be willing, if He asks, to give all for His sake, not only material things, but associations, desires, ideas,

doubts, fears, hopes, and ambitions, in fact everything. Sometimes it comes through a venture of
faith, the bold stepping out in obedience to some
call of the conscience, relying upon the Spirit to
give guidance and strength for the venture. To
some it has come when they have joyfully given
thanks in acknowledgment that some great blessing
they have received must have been a gift direct
from God Himself. Others have found it in a quiet
time of meditation, in seeming to lose self in the
Infinite, as the result of time spent in adoration of
the Spirit dwelling within. Others, again, have
found it through new light suddenly shining upon
some words of Scripture, making them live as a
personal message direct from God. Sometimes the
coming is accompanied by a manifestation of power,
or by the whole heart and mind being filled with an
ecstasy of joy entirely independent of external
surroundings ; in others it is marked by a profound
realization of the Peace which passeth all understanding. To some the realization comes so slowly
that there is no definite point which can be marked
as the time of its coming.

Whatever the cause, or the mode, of the coming
there is no doubt that the whole outlook of life is
changed ; and instead of asking God to help us in
our work, we shall begin to realize His power to
use us in *His* work.

Do remember that this realization is the gift of
God. It is not to be found by stimulating the
emotions till we persuade ourselves that we have
secured it ; it is the working of the Holy Spirit in

the heart that is ready to receive, and proves its
readiness by some act of faith.

Possibly you will think that I am making the
quest for healing appear too difficult, and beyond
the reach of ordinary people who have to live busy
lives, and have little opportunity for prayer and
meditation. This is far from my intention ; and
though I must emphasize this matter of personal
experience as the necessary aim of every Christian,
I know that God is very merciful, and looks upon
the desire of our hearts.

There is no doubt that many have been, and are
being healed, who have not yet reached the stage
of personal experience ; and have therefore not been
able to come in the fulness of faith ; but if the
desire of the heart is sincerely towards God, and if
we are honestly striving to make a venture of faith,
however feeble it may be in reality, He will accept
the little faith we are able to show. It may not be
very much ; but if, like the widow's mite, it is our
all, He will bless it and make it sufficient to meet
our need.

Now the fact that God does grant many blessings
to very imperfect ventures of faith must not tempt
us to think that the full faith, such as St. James
has in mind, is unnecessary : we must not rest till
we have found it.

" Faith is the substance of things hoped for, the
evidence of things unseen " : or, in other words, it
is the awareness of the Spiritual. Faith, therefore,
is within reach of all. It does not depend upon our
power to make ourselves believe that which is

difficult to accept ; but upon the power of the Holy
Spirit enabling us to apprehend the reality of the
Spiritual. When we speak of *our* faith we must
mean faith that is ours only in virtue of the use
that we make of it ; the faith itself is not ours ; it
is the faith of the Christ within us, for it is His
Spirit that gives to us the awareness of the reality
of the unseen.

The trouble with so many of us is, not that we
have no faith, but that we have not made use of it.
God gives us the faith ; but we have to use it, and
to go on using it till we come to rely upon it instinctively. It is the failure to realize this that causes
people to talk about *their* faith, or to bemoan the
want of it.

A man may have been endowed with a remarkable
talent for music, but that natural gift will not take
him to the front rank of musicians, unless he is
prepared to put in years of practice. So we are
endowed with the power to perceive the Spiritual ;
but that will not develop into power to rely upon
the Spiritual till we have practised using it with
the same patient perseverance as the musician.

It is useless for a man to wish that he could play
the violin like a Kreisler, if he is not willing to put
in all the necessary hours of practice, and devote
himself to the attainment of his desire. So it is
useless for us to wish that we had a faith like George
Müller, or Hudson Taylor, if we are not willing to
wait upon God as they did, and to act upon the
assurance that the Holy Spirit is dwelling in us.
There is this difference, however, that, while it is

given to few to have the natural talent of the great violinist, the Father gives the Holy Spirit to all who ask. We could not all become great violinists, because we have not the gift ; but it is open to any to become a Müller, who is willing to give himself to God as Müller did.

Now we can see what St. James means by the prayer of faith. It is coming to the Father, whom we know in Christ Jesus, not so much to ask as to receive ; or to assure Him that we are ready to receive that which we know He is ready to give.

Of course there are many things we should like to receive, without knowing whether God is willing to give, and we must therefore qualify our prayer by adding " if it be Thy will." As we are now considering the question of healing, we know that no such qualification is necessary, because He has shown to us that it is His will to heal. It is because we have this knowledge through the evidence of the Scriptures, and because we have knowledge of Him through the power of the indwelling Spirit, that we can pray the prayer of faith, the prayer which St. James assures us will bring healing to the sick.

" Whatsoever ye pray and ask for, believe that ye have received it, and ye shall have it." If our prayer is for that which we know is God's will to give, and is offered not only in the Name of Jesus, but also in the Faith of Jesus, we know that we shall receive ; so we can at once begin to give thanks. Even if the fulfilment of the promise is delayed (we shall consider possible reasons for delay later), the same faith, the Faith of Jesus, which made the prayer, will maintain the assurance till the healing is manifested, and will enable us to continue in thanksgiving, even when we do not see any visible evidence of fulfilment.

There are some who seem to regard perseverance in prayer as evidence of faith. I have heard a sufferer say, " I do believe in prayer, and I do believe that God can heal me ; I have been praying for months, and I go on praying, which I should not do if I had not got faith." I would answer such an one, that if he were really convinced of God's willingness and power to heal him, where is the necessity for such persistent prayer ? Why should he keep on asking God to give, if he is sure that He is willing to give. Does he think that he has not yet succeeded in attracting His attention to his need, or that He requires to be constantly reminded of His promise ? Would not real faith be shown rather by thanksgiving, when once the need had been carefully made known to God in prayer ? Certainly we are taught in the Gospels to continue in prayer ; but our perseverance should be in assuring God that we believe that He is looking after us, rather than in trying to persuade Him to do so.

Prayers are often spoiled by the constant repetition of details ; thus using it as an occasion for brooding over troubles, rather than the quiet, trustful, looking up to the Father, which would bring strength and comfort. The more we brood over the details, the more difficult we make healing, because the mind becomes more and more obsessed with the thought of the very thing we are longing to get rid of.

The real purpose of prayer is not to try to persuade God to do what *we* want, but so to lose ourselves in contemplation of Him, that He is able to fill our hearts with the desire to do what *He* wants. It is when we thus lose ourselves in Him, He will give to us the assurance that He is fulfilling His purpose in us ; so that our prayers for healing should not be repeated attempts to get something from Him, but quiet times of waiting upon Him, so that He may work His will in us, delivering us from the manifestation of evil which is marring the Temple of His Holy Spirit.

One of our difficulties is to pray the prayer of faith for something more than we are really able to expect. However firmly we may believe in the fact that God is able and willing to heal, it is by no means easy, till we have reached the full faith, to expect, in full assurance, complete and instantaneous healing. For example : if a person has been suffering for months, or possibly years, from a disease like arthritis, when the sufferer knows instinctively that every movement brings pain, it is difficult to eliminate this knowledge of experience. and to be able to expect complete delivery from pain in a moment. It is not only a question of the conscious mind expecting it, but the subconscious mind must expect it also ; otherwise, however boldly the sufferer may try to stretch out his limbs, there will be the lurking fear that the pain will still be there.

Now here is an opportunity for making ventures of faith. The mind may not yet be ready to expect complete delivery from pain, but it should be able to expect relief for a short time. To one suffering pain I would say : pray that the pain may be taken away for ten minutes ; and having prayed, endeavour to fix the mind on something of sufficient interest to divert it from thoughts of self ; pray for other sufferers, or read some of the psalms of praise, and you will find that relief has come. When the pain shows signs of returning, repeat the act of faith, and, as you find the reality of it, lengthen the period. I have known the pain of an abscess under a tooth relieved in this way so effectually that sleep intervened before the third period was finished. The relief, of course, will not come if one is watching, or waiting, for the pain to go. Having prayed, one must believe that the prayer will be answered, and therefore there is no need to watch for the answer. Ventures of faith of this kind will help towards the faith which will be able to expect complete healing. We must remember that the subconscious mind cannot be " bluffed," and it has no reasoning power, it works almost automatically. A fixed idea is always seeking opportunity to express itself, and once it gets started it will run its course, unless a stronger idea overwhelms it. We can see, then, that the instinctive expectation of pain can only be overcome by the Truth ; when the Holy Spirit

makes the Truth of Divine Healing live in the heart
as well as in the mind, and acceptance of the Truth
has been proved by ventures of faith. It is not
sufficient to say that we believe, if we are conscious
of a lurking fear in " the back of the mind." If
that is so we must not only say, " Lord, I believe,"
but add, like the father of the lunatic boy, " help
Thou mine unbelief," handing over the subconscious
fear to Him, in confidence that the Holy Spirit can
overcome it. Then we shall be able to receive,
because we shall be able to expect.

One of the surest proofs of the evil nature of
sickness is that it frequently makes prayer very
difficult, if not altogether impossible. In such cases
the prayer of faith must be offered by the relatives
and friends rather than by the patient.

In many cases it is easier for the friends to have
more faith than the patient, and thus to pray more
effectually, because their minds are not so filled
with the consciousness of pain or infirmity. On
the other hand, when one who is dearly loved is
being prayed for, there is a great risk that the very
intensity of the love will be the cause of great
anxiety, and the patient will be surrounded with
fear instead of faith. I shall have more to say on
this subject in a later chapter, but I must call
attention to the danger now. When we are praying
for others we must do all we can to avoid anxiety,
and above all refrain from letting our minds be
filled with the thought of the suffering. We must
surround the sufferer with thoughts of health, not

of infirmity, and as we bring them to Christ we must believe that He is healing, not merely pitying, them.

Some time ago there was recorded in the *Science of Thought Review* the case of a woman whose ear-drum had perished, and the bone surrounding it was soft. Twelve months afterwards, her doctor was amazed to find a perfect ear-drum. Her daughter, instead of praying for her in pity, with the thought of the infirmity in her mind, kept before her the thought of the ear as it should be in the perfection which God had planned. Her prayer of faith had thus been the channel through which the healing Grace could flow.

I cannot help feeling that it is a mistake to give minute details of a patient's infirmity when prayers are being offered by a group of Intercessors. Something more than a bare name is necessary in order to give the sense of personality, but the last thing we want to do is to fix our minds on the infirmity. Sometimes people will tell you that they cannot pray effectually, unless they know what is the matter with the patient. I believe that to be a mistaken idea; in fact the value of the prayer is often weakened, if not entirely destroyed, by such knowledge, because, if the disease happens to be one which is generally regarded as incurable, or extremely serious, the prayer is liable to be one of hope, or even despair, rather than of faith. Our prayers for others must be positive rather than negative, dwelling on the perfection to which God wills to bring them, rather than on the imperfection which exists. There can be no higher thought than to pray that the sufferer be made Christ-like, in body as well as in soul; it covers all the needs of humanity, and leaves the issue with God.

There is really no need to tell God what we think is the matter, or what we think would be best for the sufferer; He knows far better than we do How many strange prayers must have been offered up, when people have been earnestly praying for the healing of some trouble which does not exist, misled by a wrong diagnosis.

The true purpose of intercession is to offer ourselves as channels of God's Grace. When we speak of Christ as our Intercessor, we do not mean that He is standing between us and an angry God, pleading for mercy: but that He, our Redeemer, Who by His Passion has broken down the barrier which sin has raised up, is standing between God and ourselves as the connecting-link, or the channel through which the Father's Love may flow freely to His children. When we act as intercessors we are forming another link in the chain, or offering our hearts as channels, through which the Healing Love may be directed to those for whom we are praying. We put, as it were, one hand in the Hand of Jesus, and the other in the hand of our friend, believing that the Love can flow through us to him. Let us therefore take care that there is nothing in our hearts to hinder the flow.

I have tried various methods of intercession, and have come to the conclusion that the best of all is that which we use daily in our own little chapel. First we read out the names of those for whom we seek help, without any attempt to explain what we think to be the matter, or what we recommend. We then spend time in silence, believing that God is using our hearts as channels of His Grace, so that He can accomplish His purpose, which must be better than anything we could suggest.

Such intercession cannot be fruitless. We are not asking God to do something, with the possibility of doubt as to whether He has heard our prayer, or is willing to answer it ; but are yielding ourselves to Him, that He may use us in the fulfilment of His purpose. We may not be able to measure the result, any more than you can measure the growth of a tree from day to day ; but as you know that every day the sun has shone upon the tree, some growth must have taken place ; so you know that every time you have yielded your heart to God as the channel of His Grace, the sunshine of His Love has been shining upon the sufferer for whom you have been seeking His help.

There is no question, therefore, of thinking that it is useless to continue to pray for a person when our prayer does not seem to have been answered, because we know that God is using us ; and if we continue to give ourselves for His use, the growth must be going on, however imperceptibly ; but of course we must take care that our hearts are free channels, and not clogged with doubts or fears as to the issue.

Remember the promise, " The prayer of faith

shall save him that is sick, and the Lord will raise him up."

The Prayer of Faith offered by Intercessors is of supreme importance in connection with mental suffering. We can have no doubt that Christ's Healing is for every affliction to which man is subject, in mind and body : so that whether the affliction of the mind be caused by some disease affecting the brain, or possession by some power of evil, it must come within the scheme of Redemption. Among the signs that follow belief, our Lord promised " In my Name they shall cast out devils " ; so we have the assurance that the Ministry of Healing is to bring deliverance to the mentally possessed, as well as to the mentally diseased. Here, then, are many who are quite unable to pray for themselves and therefore need all the help that can be given them through intercession, which must be intercession of the right kind, sending only the highest thoughts of God's healing Love, and content to go on, in patient perseverance, for long periods without the encouragement of visible improvement. You may think that I am showing a want of faith in the power of the Healing Christ in stating that the healing of such cases may take a long time. It is not that I have any doubts about the power to heal : it is that circumstances make it difficult. It is an unavoidable necessity that mental cases should be under control, and therefore gathered together in Institutions provided for them. I can think of nothing more calculated to hinder the healing than the atmosphere that is inevitable where many such cases are in close association. I see no possibility of any other arrangement, so that there is all the greater need for an abundance of prayer help for these unfortunate people. The Prayer Union for Mental Sufferers is doing a great work in organizing intercession, and is now seeking to arrange for prayer help for the inmates of the Asylums throughout the country. The idea is to get the largest possible number of intercessors in the neighbourhood of these Institutions to undertake the work of regular, and systematic, intercession for the sufferers, endeavouring to surround each of the Institutions with a circle of intercessors.

Here is an opportunity for good work; and any who feel moved to help in it should communicate with the Secretary of the Prayer Union for Mental Sufferers, 19, Pembridge Crescent, W.11.

CHAPTER V

OBEDIENCE

HOLY SCRIPTURE makes it abundantly clear that disease is an evil thing, and the product of evil. It shows us equally clearly that, being evil, deliverance from it is one of the inestimable benefits of our Lord's Passion ; and therefore, that healing is given in response to faith in the Name of Jesus Christ.

We must remember also that Health is the Law of God's Kingdom, depending upon the observance of His commands.

We see, therefore, that though healing is given to faith, the maintenance of health depends upon obedience. " Sin no more," said our Lord, " lest a worse thing befall thee."

Let no man suppose that Divine Healing is an easy way of saving doctors' bills ; or is likely to be given in order that he may go on his own way forgetful of the Lord who healed him.

Divine Healing, or Divinely given Health, is a way of life, and must mean that the seeker thereof is determined to live day by day dependent upon God, seeking each day sufficient for the day, and content to leave to-morrow to the Father's care.

In the first place, we approach Christ for healing because we are attracted by the knowledge of His compassion. We hope that, because His compassion is so boundless, He will have mercy even on us, and deliver us from the sore burden of our affliction. As we approach nearer we realize that we are coming to something far bigger: that the Father Himself is not only willing, but actually longing, to heal us, in order that He may make us fit for His service. So we see that healing means not only the relief of the pain or infirmity which distresses us, but the healing of the whole being—spirit, soul, and body. We have no right to expect healing by the Grace of God if we are not willing to surrender our whole being to Him, and to seek the cleansing of the soul, as well as the healing of the mind and body.

I knew a man once who had been suffering for a long time from acute indigestion. He had been to several doctors, who had tried various remedies without any effect. His trouble got worse and worse, until he could hardly carry on his work. At last he went to another doctor, who was not content till he had made a thorough examination of him. He found that the primary cause was eye-strain, which had affected his nervous system. The strain was relieved by the use of suitable glasses, and normal health gradually returned.

When we come to God for healing we must let Him diagnose our trouble; for the physical sickness, from which we are so anxious to be relieved, may be caused by some wrong mental outlook, some fear or anxiety; or possibly a wrong habit; or some unrepented sin. We must be ready to let the Spirit of Truth search our hearts, and bring to our conscious mind anything that He sees in need of cleansing, alteration, or readjustment.

If we are not willing to do this, not only have we no right to expect healing, but we are making it practically impossible; because the Grace of God works from within. If you had an abscess on your hand it might be healed by the outward application of fomentations, and afterwards ointments; the whole treatment being entirely local. But if you are looking to Christ for healing, the healing will come from within, by His sending such a flow of life to the afflicted part that the disease will be driven out by the force of the life stream flowing to it, by the recuperative power of the body working at its fullest strength. You may say that this is simply a mental process, which can be produced by the will, or even the hopeful outlook of the optimist, or by the power of suggestion. That might be true to a great extent; but there is no certainty about it, for it is not every one who is open to the power of suggestion, and few have the necessary force of will. If, on the other hand, you are seeking healing through Christ, the natural recuperative power is controlled by His Spirit, so that nothing can withstand it. It follows, then, that if we want the Spirit to take control, He must have complete possession of the heart ; and we must be prepared to live in complete submission and obedience to His will.

When we come to Christ for healing we must put ourselves entirely into His keeping, and seek to be made what He would have us to be, and not merely to be delivered from the troubles which are apparent to ourselves. As we have just seen, it is more than likely that the ailment, from which we seek to be healed, was caused by something far more deeply seated ; or if not actually caused by it, or held by it, we were exposed to its attack by some wrong state of mind.

Dr. Edward Bach actually traces cause and effect. He says : "Pride, which is arrogance and rigidity of mind, will give rise to those diseases which produce rigidity and stiffness of the body. . . . The penalties of hate are loneliness, violent uncontrollable temper, mental nerve storms, and conditions of hysteria. The diseases of introspection—neurosis, neurasthenia, and similar conditions—which rob life of so much enjoyment, are caused by excessive Self-love." St. James, therefore, bids us not only offer the prayer of faith ; but also confess our sins one to another.

There can be no doubt about it, the root and strength of disease is sin. Sin is an ugly word, so is disease an ugly thing; it is no good mincing matters, we must face them both.

Possibly we need to widen our definition of sin ; and to give up limiting our conception of it to the breaking of the Ten Commandments in their most obvious interpretation.

The sins we commit in word and deed are probably a very small proportion of the sins of thought ; but the absence of outward expression is no guarantee that the state of the mind is not sinful. Sin is the rejection, not only of God's Commands, but of His Love, and of His Guidance. Any turning away from Him, any attempt to act in our own wisdom and strength, is in the nature of sin ; and the sooner we are honest enough to admit it, the better.

God is Love, therefore any state of mind which is unloving, hinders His complete possession of us. An unforgiving spirit, bitterness of heart, slander, jealousy, contempt, criticism, or the repetition of unkind stories about our neighbours, especially behind their backs, are all negations of love, and therefore sin in the sight of God. Fear is sin because it is the refusal to accept God's word. If we really believed the promises of God, there would be no fear, except that of having to do, or face, things we do not like ; which indicates the sin of self-will, or unwillingness to surrender. Yet how many there are who regard fear as though it were some natural and, therefore, excusable weakness, instead of confessing it as the sin of unbelief. At the root of most of our sins is self-conscious vanity. It is the cause of jealousy, untruthfulness, and self-pity. It is behind that fear of ridicule which is so voluble in self-justification ; the strength of which can be seen in the fact that probably the majority of us would rather be thought to have done something wrong, than to have made ourselves ridiculous.

We need to be honest, and to give these things their right names, instead of labelling them as difficulties, or limitations. It sounds much better to excuse our unreadiness to carry on the Master's work in the way He wants, by saying that we are hindered by a natural shyness, rather than by the self-conscious fear of being thought awkward or foolish. So too it is much more self-satisfying to think that our fears are due to a nervous disposition, instead of our failure to trust God's Love, and to surrender ourselves to Him. When we find ourselves terribly hurt by adverse criticism, or unkind acts, it is far more soothing to attribute our wounded feelings to the sensitiveness of our nature, than to admit that our vanity has received a rude shock.

Dishonesty is a very elastic term with many people. They are horrified at the idea of taking away that which belongs to another; but see nothing wrong in preventing him from getting that which is his due. There are many who would not dream of robbing a neighbour of half a sovereign; but would have no compunction in selling, for a sovereign, an article which they knew to be worth less than half that sum. A certain element of risk is often regarded as a legitimate excuse for dishonesty, such as trying to evade customs duties, or travelling without a ticket, or even presenting inaccurate income-tax returns. To insinuate a lie, or to allow a lie to be believed by keeping silence, is just as dishonest as telling a lie direct; though the world may not regard it so.

There is no greater bar to healing than impurity of thought. Acts of impurity are self-condemned, but there are many to whom the very idea of such an act would be abhorrent, who nevertheless find sensual pleasure in sights or books that stimulate the passions, without realizing that, by so doing, they are keeping the Holy Spirit from complete possession of the heart.

The command to do unto others as we would they should do unto us, opens up a vast field in which most of us frequently act against the highest principles of Love. There is no need for me to mention obvious cases, for the simple reason that they are obvious, but it is good for us to have our eyes opened to those which are less noticeable.

Have we ever thought it necessary to confess the distress we may have caused some fellow-traveller, or fellow-member of a community, by our selfish insistence on the amount of air, or warmth, we consider necessary, without any regard to the feelings of others. Self comes up everywhere, and the greater the place it occupies in our lives the less room there is for the Spirit of Christ.

One of the most soul-destroying forms of self is self-pity; and who among us can claim to be entirely free from it? It urges us to claim some infirmity, real, or imaginary, as the excuse for our failures: it delights to nurse some grievance, and make us regard ourselves as martyrs, thereby causing us to become irritable and sulky.

Most of us, who have had long illnesses, have experienced the difficulty of taking up again the responsibilities of life, and forgoing the attentions and considerations which were shown us in the time of our weakness. It is one of the greatest difficulties we have to face, and at times it seems almost impossible to make a patient realize that the real cause of delayed healing is that he really does not want to get well. He will tell you that he is most anxious to be healed, and no doubt it is true, up to a point. He longs to be freed from pain and suffering, but, all unconsciously perhaps, he clings to the attentions to which he has grown accustomed. This may be caused by vanity, because such attentions minister to the self-esteem; and many who cannot command attention in any other way, will do so by claiming the sympathy due to the sick. Frequently it is caused by self-pity, which makes its victim feel that he ought not be expected to undertake the full duties of life. These two evils between them have been responsible for many lifelong invalids, and " malades imaginaires "; so that God has been defrauded, not only of the full service they should have rendered Him, but also of the service of those whom their selfishness has kept in waiting attendance upon them.

The willing sufferings of Christ for our sake are the strongest indictment of self-pity. It certainly is not Christ-like to make our feelings an excuse for shirking our duty; thus putting a heavier burden upon others, who may be suffering far more than we are. Of course I am not thinking of times of real illness, or infirmity, but of those minor troubles, which self-pity loves to magnify out of all proportion.

What, after all, are our sufferings compared to the sufferings of our Lord ? Satan is always ready to use self-pity as the means of entry into the heart of man ; and so has tempted some to think that the intensity, and duration, of their own agony has exceeded that of Jesus. Let such an one ask himself if he has ever, or could ever, experience a fractional part of the mental sufferings of Jesus ; the Incarnation of Love, rejected by those He died to save ; or the Spiritual suffering during those hours of darkness, when the barrier raised by our sins was allowed to come between Him and the Father's Love.

Sometimes self-pity tempts us to a state of resentment against God. We have honestly tried to make a venture of faith, and instead of getting the help we felt that we had a right to expect, everything seems to have gone against us. We are tempted to blame God, because we fail to realize that He cannot always give the blessings promised to faith, till the faith has been tested. It would be easy enough to claim faith, if everything came just when we want it : faith means holding on to the promise of God, regardless of circumstances. So far from proving that God has forgotten us, these trials of faith are really proofs that He regards us as worth training for His service.

If we want the Spirit of Christ to possess us, we must face these things ; and if we are honestly determined to do so, we may take it as a very useful guide, that the faults which we find particularly irritating in other people are probably those which find a place in our own character. This is a fact admitted by most psychologists. There is no need to discuss the psychological reason for this : it proves itself over and over again in practice ; so we cannot afford to ignore it, however distasteful or humiliating it may be. The very fact that we may be inclined to resent it, goes a long way towards proving that is true.

If we want to receive God's blessing we have got to be perfectly honest with Him : He cannot possess us until we are ; and until He possesses us He cannot work His will in us. There must be no secret chambers in the heart, to which we are unwilling to admit Him ; no corners which we are trying to shield from the light of His Presence. The honest desire of the heart must be for perfect purity, perfect truth, and perfect love. If we find the desire lacking, we must pray the Father to overwhelm any contrary or rebellious desires, by the power of His Holy Spirit. When our weaknesses are revealed to us, we must set about getting rid of them, and we must realize that this is beyond the power of the human will. The will may serve to keep a fault in check for a time ; but the will, being an effort of the conscious mind, grows tired, while the evil habit, or rather the thought behind it, is a fixed idea in the subconscious mind, which never grows tired, but is always watching for an opportunity to express itself. Take, for example, the sin of impurity of thought, whether or no it ever expresses itself in action. Nothing is harder to check by the power of the human will. When conscience convicts of its presence, it is of little use to pray merely for strength to overcome the temptation. We must go deeper than that, and pray that the desire may be rooted out of the heart ; or that the heart may be filled with such a strong desire to maintain the body as the Temple of the Holy Spirit, that all impure desires will be overwhelmed by it. So with all wrong thoughts which lead to sin, from which possibly some may have despaired of ever being delivered ; we must take them to God for Him to root out the desire ; without waiting till such times as they are threatening to lead us into sin.

We can never have that peace of mind in which the Spirit of the Healing Christ can do His work in us, as long as we are conscious of some unrighted wrong. St. James is emphasizing a very important truth when he urges us to confess our faults one to another. To make restitution, or to acknowledge that we have been unjust or unkind, is by no means easy ; but the greater the difficulty, the stronger the proof of the vanity which will not let us acknowledge our wrong-doings ; and that vanity has got to go, before Christ can take complete possession. There is nothing more potent in uprooting it, than confession to the person we have wronged.

While we are considering the subject of wrong thoughts, we must remember the necessity of being on our guard against the danger of getting into a groove, as nothing is more conducive to selfishness. It is so easy to get into the way of thinking that certain conditions of life, or certain articles of diet, are so absolutely necessary to our existence, that we are apt to demand them, without regard to the inconvenience we may be causing other people. Similarly, we may become so convinced of the rightness of our own opinions, that we try to impose them upon others, and become intolerant, and possibly contemptuous of those who dare to disagree. It is well to remember the warning, that such hardness of mind means laying ourselves open to the diseases which cause hardness in the body also.

To sum up what I have been attempting to make clear, the position is this :

It is of little use to come to God merely to ask for the healing of some bodily infirmity. We must be prepared to let Him decide what really is the matter with us, and be willing to have the whole of our life reconstructed, and reorganized, if it is necessary in His sight. We must pray that He will, by the light of the Spirit of Truth, reveal to us what there is in heart, or mind, that must be put right before the physical infirmity can be healed. We must be filled with the desire to be used in His service, to live in obedience to His commands, dependent upon Him day by day for all we need in spirit, soul, and body.

I do not mean that we have to achieve all this

before we can be healed; if that were so, who would be healed?

What I do mean is, that we must let Him, Who reads the secrets of our hearts, see that this is our honest desire. Does it seem too high a standard for ordinary human beings? After all, it is only what we imply when we express the desire to be made Christ-like.

I am not suggesting that any one of us could approach anywhere near it by the strength of his own will, but that it is what the Holy Spirit can do in us, if we will let Him.

CHAPTER VI

TO THE GLORY OF GOD

THERE is still another question we must consider, and that is our motive. It is not sufficient merely to desire healing in order that we may be relieved of pain, or disability.

Take the analogy of sin. Do we seek the forgiveness of sins merely for our own safety? Nay, surely it is that our hearts being cleansed from sin, God may fill us with His Spirit, and use us in His service. True repentance, therefore, must be based on sorrow for having rejected the Love of God, for having hurt His Love by our sin, and not sorrow at having got ourselves into trouble, or having injured our self-esteem. So too the desire for the healing of the body must not be limited to the consideration of our own comfort, however natural that desire may be. We must seek the Glory of God, and that our bodies may be made once again usable in His service. So the sorrow for sickness must not be only self-pity, but sorrow that the Temple has become defiled. There is a case on record of a woman, who had suffered for a long time from a very painful disease. She had prayed earnestly, and constantly, for relief ; but without result. At last she was moved to seek first the realization of Christ, and she prayed that it might be granted to her to have the power to realize His Presence. She was ready to endure anything if that could be given her, she would even welcome the pain, if that could be the means of such realization. From that moment the pain was eased, and healing commenced. As long as she sought only her own comfort, she could receive nothing ; but as soon as she put Christ first, she was able to receive all.

God glorifies Himself in healing His children, and we must seek His glory.

In the story of the Ten Lepers this is strongly emphasized. The nine who did not return, are generally held up to us as examples of ingratitude ; but our Lord did not so accuse them. He expressed surprise that there was but one who returned to *give glory to God*. There would have been nothing very remarkable in the Samaritan being more grateful than the Jews ; in fact he might have been considered to have had more reason for thankfulness, in that he, being a Samaritan, had been cleansed by a Jewish Healer. There was, however, something very remarkable in the fact that the Samaritan, rather than the Jews, perceived that God was glorified by his healing. Doubtless the nine were thankful also, but, so anxious were they to enjoy their newly recovered health, and to get to their homes and families, that they

gave no thought to the higher meaning of their
release from the manifestation of evil. The
Samaritan put the glory of God before his own
satisfaction.

Is it not an inspiring thought that the Glory of
the Almighty God can be manifested in us : that
He is willing, nay desirous, to deliver us from
every manifestation of evil in soul, and body, so
that He may show forth His Love in us, and
through us.

Preaching, without practice, is not going to
convert the world ; in fact it is more likely to repel,
because it arouses criticism. When men can see
the teaching of Christ lived out by those who
profess to be His followers, they will be drawn to
seek the same Grace. So too, when men see that
those who look to Him as their Healer are delivered
from their infirmities, they will be drawn to seek
the same deliverance.

We can often see in children a likeness to
their parents ; sometimes in similarity of feature ;
sometimes in character. Should not the children
of God, created in His image, reveal some
likeness to Him. Again, we can often see, by
the appearance of children, the kind of home
from which they come. Some, though obviously
poor, are neat and clean, with clothes carefully
mended, and cared for ; while others, though
showing fewer signs of poverty, are dirty and
unkempt. Should not the children of God, that
is to say, those who claim their heritage, be able
to bear witness that the Father is proving His

Love by His care for body and soul; thus
manifesting His Glory in them. That is worth
more than all the preaching; for it is that which
compels those who observe it to seek the same
source of Grace.

A good deal of harm is often done by over-zealous
people who will, in season and out of season, talk
of having received Divine Healing, before the
healing is complete. They honestly desire to bear
witness; but they forget that the world demands
facts, and is not likely to be convinced by being
told that a certain person is feeling better. To
claim healing is to invite critical observation,
and if it is still apparent that there are con-
siderable limitations, the claim is ridiculed;
but when healing is apparent, and former known
limitations have been removed, friends and
acquaintances will inquire after the source of the
regained strength. They will then be in a recep-
tive, instead of a critical, frame of mind, and
anxious to learn; so the witness will be accepted,
because the proof is undeniable; and God will be
glorified.

Possibly it may be thought that to insist on the
necessity of putting the Glory of God first, is to
encourage hypocrisy. You may ask: "Am I to
say that I desire to be healed for God's Glory, when
all the time I know in my heart that what I
really want is to be freed from some racking
pain, or some infirmity which hinders me from
earning my living: surely it is only human nature

to seek first, relief from suffering." It is not really a question of desire. Human nature is well endowed with courage; and does not shrink from pain, if the cause is deemed worth the endurance.

Think what sufferings have been willingly faced, and cheerfully endured, by men and women, in time of war; by explorers; or mountaineers; or by those who strive to win wealth in perilous ways. Or think again what many of us have been content to suffer in the cause of sport, in hard training or racing, or playing games which often result in serious accidents. Think again what women, throughout the ages, have smilingly endured in the cause of fashion, when, for instance, wasp waists were the approved style; or when feet are forced into shoes too small to accommodate them. All these sufferings have been borne because the object has been deemed worth the sacrifice. So too have countless thousands endured the sufferings of persecution, or martyrdom, because their love for the Crucified Saviour made them willing to bear anything for His sake. Love is always willing to make sacrifice, and to bear suffering; and where there is real fellowship with Christ, there will be the love which will make suffering for His sake worth while.

Now you will probably say that I am contradicting myself. First, I emphasize the need of seeking healing for the Glory of God, and now bid you suffer patiently for Christ's sake. If God is willing to heal, why is it necessary for us to be willing to go on suffering? It does sound like a paradox, but it is not so really.

If I am unwilling to suffer the pain for Christ's sake, it must be because I am anxious to get rid of it for my own sake; and thus it is obvious that I am not putting God first. If, on the other hand, I am willing to suffer for Christ's sake, I am no longer desiring healing merely for my own comfort; and thus able to consider impartially how I can best glorify God.

We shall find also that this is true psychologically. If my main object is to get rid of the suffering, my mind becomes so filled with the thought of it, not unmixed with fear, that, although my great desire is to be freed, I am in reality holding on to the realization of the pain, so that it cannot be taken away; but if I can make up my mind that I can endure it, I am really letting go my hold, so that the Grace of God can heal me.

The same principle holds good in seeking healing for others. Are we asking that they may be healed to the Glory of God; or because we love them so much, that we cannot bear to contemplate the possibility of losing them? We must be willing to lose them for Christ's sake, before we can pray that God will glorify Himself in healing them. If our one desire is the satisfaction of our own love, we are so afraid that the loved one may be taken from us, that we are surrounding him with fear and anxiety, which not only destroys our own faith, but the faith of the patient also. A feeling of resignation is not sufficient. To be ready to say, " God's will be done," if we cannot get our own way, is not by any means a willing surrender of our loved one to Christ. Is this surrender too difficult ? Is it less difficult to surrender him to the skill of the surgeon, than into the Hands of the Christ Who bore his sickness upon the Cross ?

Whether the healing we are seeking is for ourselves, or for others, the whole matter of surrender depends upon our love for Christ : and a love sufficient for these things must depend upon knowledge—not the intellectual knowledge of the historical Jesus, but the personal experience of fellowship with Him The living Christ must be a reality to us before we can have for Him a love strong enough to make us willing to suffer for His sake. I have already tried to show how that experience may be found : here I would only point to this additional proof of the necessity of finding it.

You may wonder, perhaps, if you have really found it, or not. Sometimes you think that you have, at other times you are not so sure. Here is no mean test. If you are ready to suffer willingly for His sake, and to put the Glory of God before all else in life, I think that there is no doubt that you have found it. The more we realize such fellowship, the stronger must grow the love ; growing till it far exceeds the love of wealth, or success, or self-glorification, or anything the world can offer.

When love such as that is filling the heart, there will be no shadow of hypocrisy in the declaration that you are seeking healing first and foremost for the Glory of Almighty God.

If we are seeking healing for the Glory of God, we may expect His work to be done perfectly. We are inclined to regard healing as a patching up, rather than a renewal. If we have a manufactured article which is wearing out, we have it mended: if it is beyond mending we have to *replace* it ; we cannot *renew* it. If it has been mended there is probably a lurking fear that it may give way again in the same place. So with the body. When some ailment, specially if it be one commonly regarded as chronic, has been healed, there is often the fear that the healing has been in the nature of a " patching up," rather than a renewal of the damaged tissues.

Christ can make all things new. If we put first His Glory, and give ourselves entirely into His keeping, He can create in us a new " heart " in which the old fears have no place ; He can print in that heart the image of perfection which is God's plan for us ; and He can rebuild the damaged cells and tissues in the likeness to that plan. I know of the case of a child, who had a very severe attack of pneumonia in one of his lungs. He was healed in answer to prayer ; and twelve months after the attack, the doctor was unable to discover which lung had been affected. Christ's healing was perfect. Seek His Glory, and He will glorify Himself in you. Do not limit Him by expecting only a partial healing: let thoughts of perfection fill your mind, and He will manifest that perfection in you.

CHAPTER VII

DIVINE HEALING AND MEDICINE

NO book on Divine Healing could be complete without attempting to face the question of the relation between the Church's Ministry of Healing and Medical Science.

There can be no doubt that the work of the doctors is abundantly blessed by God; or that suffering humanity owes a very great debt to the skill and devotion of the members of the Medical Profession : but, on the other hand, there are many who feel that they are lacking in faith if they make use of medicinal remedies.

This feeling has nothing in common with the attitude of " Christian Science " towards doctors, and their work, which is based upon a denial of the reality of material things. No believer in Divine Healing, which recognizes the terrible reality of disease, can have anything but admiration for the fight which the Medical Profession is making against the evil.

The question is simply this : Should the believer in Divine Healing take medicine, or should he trust entirely to the power of the Healing Christ ? I believe that the answer to the question is, that it depends entirely upon the stage of spiritual development to which we have attained. If our personal experience of the abiding Presence of our Lord is as real to us as His visible Presence was real to those who beheld Him in Galilee, then I cannot see that medicine should be any more necessary to us than it was to those who were healed by His touch, or by His spoken word alone.

If, on the other hand, we have not yet reached that stage, we cannot afford to do without it.

It is useless to try experiments ; such as trying to do without medicine because we think that we *ought* to be able to get healing direct from God without it. We must go on using medical means until we have something better to take their place : experiments will only end in disaster.

Let me explain my meaning by a simple example. Suppose that you have been in the habit of taking some drug to induce sleep. You feel that the time has come when you ought to make an effort to give it up. You say, " To-night, I will *try* to do without it." Very likely you will give in before the night is over, and take your dose ; or, if your will is strong enough to enable you to keep to your resolve, you will reach the morning with nerves severely tried, after a night of little, or no sleep. The very fact of saying that you would *try* admitted the subconscious possibility, or even expectation of failure ; and the failure followed as a matter of course. Before you can give up the drug—unless, of course, it has been merely a temporary expedient,

used in a time of physical weakness from which you
have quite recovered—you must have something to
take its place. Affirm your belief that the Holy
Spirit is dwelling within you ; if you do not feel
quite sure of it, remind yourself that the fact of His
indwelling depends not upon your feelings, but upon
the promise of the Son of God. In the power of
that affirmation you can say with real meaning,
" Because I know that the Holy Spirit is dwelling
within me, and that the fruit of His indwelling is
peace, I know that by the Grace of God I can realize
His peace." Pray for that realization—wait upon
God to receive the gift—give thanks to prove that
you believe that you have received it ; then affirm
that, because you know that the Peace of God is
possessing you, it will be quite unnecessary to take
any sleeping-draught. If the whole being is filled
with peace, sleep will come naturally ; and instead
of giving up an aid which you are afraid you will
miss, you are giving it up because you know that
you have something far better in its place.

While on the subject of sleep, perhaps a digression
may be permissible. It is a great mistake to pray
for sleep, however much we may long for it. The
special effort of prayer is an acknowledgment of
fear that you will not sleep. Why the need of a
special effort, if that fear were not hovering in the
background ? Thus the special effort, in giving
recognition to the fear, strengthens it, and renders
the possibility of sleep more remote. What you
should pray for is, grace to be able to realize the

peace, which is yours because it is the fruit of the
Spirit dwelling in you. Sleep is a natural thing,
and will come naturally, if spirit, mind, and body
are full of peace.

To return to our subject. I have used this
question of the sleeping-draught to illustrate a
principle. Do not be tempted to make experiments. We cannot afford to forgo the use of
material remedies, till we have something better
to put in their place. Here, however, we must be
careful not to confuse experiments with ventures of
faith. What I am condemning is the attempt to
make a venture merely because we think we ought
to try, while we are half-expecting to fail. The
venture of faith is a venture which we are quite
convinced ought to succeed, because we are relying
not on our own strength, but on the Grace of God,
and claiming the fulfilment of His promise.

I hope that I have now made my meaning clear,
when I say that the use of medicinal aids depends
upon the stage we have reached in spiritual development. It is simply a matter of faith. We cannot
do without the material aid as long as there is any
lurking fear that we are putting aside something
that would help towards recovery : but, as long as
we use medicines, we must use them as the gift of
God, and ask His blessing upon them, in fact " say
grace " over them as we should over food. There
must be no question of using medicine for safety, in
case the Divine Healing should fail. The Rev. J. T.

Butlin, in his *Handbook of Divine Healing*, mentions
such a case, where the patient was receiving ministration from him, and at the same time holding fast
to his medicines. Nothing wrong in that, if he had
been using the medicine in the belief that it was
the way appointed for his healing. Mr. Butlin
perceived that, in this case, he was really trying
both methods, for fear one should fail; and merely
hoping that one or the other would prove successful.
He told him, therefore, that he must choose between
them. The patient gave up his medicine, put his
whole trust in God, and at once began to recover
his health.

We are sometimes met with the contention that
since God has given to man the knowledge of the
use of drugs, and skill in surgery, this is the appointed
way of healing for this generation; and therefore
we ought not attempt to seek healing in any other
way; suggesting that to do so is to despise God's
gifts. It is strange to find preachers of the Gospel
asking us to believe that progress in faith can
involve the neglect of that which is definitely
spiritual, in favour of material means. How hopeless is their argument in the face of facts. Thank
God for the doctors, and all they are doing in
fighting disease; but, at its best, medical science is
a very poor substitute for the Healing of Christ
through His Church. If Christ's healing were no
longer for the use of man I should not be writing
these words; as Medical Science has not yet discovered any way to combat sleepy sickness: and

it was solely the Grace of God, using Mr. James
Moore Hickson as His channel, that healed me from
that disease seven years ago ; when the doctors
admitted that they were helpless. Some day
probably the means of curing cancer and consump-
tion will be discovered, but at present there is no
certain cure ; and thousands die from these diseases
every year. The number would be larger still, but
for the fact that more and more are turning to
Christ as their Healer, and finding that He is still
the same as when He healed the sick in Galilee.

Undoubtedly medical means and skill are God's
gift to suffering humanity ; but not given to take
the place of healing through faith in Christ. Rather
one would imagine they are given because the
loving Father will not leave His suffering children
without help, in an age when His Church is failing
to carry out Her Lord's command.

No one can doubt the enormous part the use of
vaccine and serums have played in the fight against
disease. Is it not a strange thing that we should
have to fight disease by inoculating disease, when
the Healing Christ is willing to cast it out by the
power of His Love ? Which would you rather
have, the Divine Life of the Son of God filling spirit,
soul, and body ; or goodness knows how many
million bacilli forced into your blood ? Which,
think you, is God's way ? Will the Father be
offended if you turn from the bacilli, to accept the
Divine Life of His Son ? And is healing through
Christ less His gift than the drugs ?

If we are still unable to reach the stage in which

we can dispense with doctors and medicines, we must be careful of the place we give them. The doctor tends us, but it is God alone Who can heal us. We must use the doctor as God's minister to the body, asking God to *use* him rather than to *help* him.

There is a very prevalent idea that St. Luke accompanied St. Paul, during part of his missionary journeys, as his medical attendant. The only ground for such an assumption is the generally accepted idea that medical aid is an absolute necessity. Because most of us were brought up to regard it as such, we have just taken it for granted that St. Luke, being a doctor, travelled with St. Paul in that capacity. There is no record that he ever ministered to St. Paul; in fact, as we have already noted, there is abundant evidence that St. Paul looked direct to God for healing: moreover, when the sick folk in the island of Malta were brought for healing, they were brought to St. Paul, and not to the physician. Surely such healing as St. Luke is most likely to have done after he became an Evangenst, must have been accomplished by the Grace of the Healing Christ, rather than by the use of drugs.

Sometimes we are accused of trying to do the doctors "out of their job." One might just as reasonably say that of those who are engaged in the research for the preventives of disease. Doctors will always find plenty of work till the whole nation turns to God, and every individual man and woman is filled with the Spirit of Christ. Even though we may now no longer feel the need of drugs or medicines, we should most of us look to the doctor as the expert adviser in the things of the body; as we should look to the priest, or the minister, for advice in spiritual matters.

For instance, a person with diabetes, however strong his faith in Christ's Healing, would want to know what foods should be avoided till the healing be complete. We certainly should seek the doctor's aid for the setting of a broken bone; or to put stitches in a gaping wound.

Taking the Medical and Nursing Professions together, I suppose that there is no body of men and women in the world exhibiting a higher standard of self-sacrificing devotion to duty in their work for suffering humanity. I can only wish that all would realize, as so many do, that they are not only striving to overcome disease, and to relieve the suffering, but are fellow-workers with God in fighting against evil. There would then be a much closer co-operation between doctors and clergy, which is what we seek. I was once asked to go and minister to a lady who was making little headway after two serious operations. I rejoiced greatly to find that, not only was it the doctor's wish that his patient should seek spiritual help, but that he himself wished to be present at the Anointing. I need hardly add that the patient took a turn for the better the same evening, and made rapid progress towards recovery.

I can fully understand the unwillingness of doctors to invite the co-operation of clergy who depress their patients by talking in a gloomy way about death, or the necessity of bearing patiently the cross which (they say) God has put upon the sufferer ; or who pay long visits with apparently no conception of what a sick person is able to endure : but there can be no doubt that they will always welcome the co-operation of those who can give their patients new hope and courage, because they recognize the supreme importance of the mental outlook, even if still unconvinced of the power of Spiritual healing.

CHAPTER VIII

MAINLY PRACTICAL

LET us now see where we stand.

You are anxious to seek healing from God. You feel moved to seek healing through the Ministry of the Church; and you want to make the best possible preparation. You will have realized that the first thing necessary is to make full confession to God of any sins, or sinful desires, which hinder perfect fellowship with Him. The completeness of your confession will depend, of course, upon the nature of your infirmity, and the effect it has upon the power to think. A person suffering from neurosis, or neurasthenia, must not probe into the past; nor must one who is very ill strive to force his mind to think deeply, even if it might seem possible to do so. In such cases a sincere desire for amendment, and determination to make complete surrender of the whole life to God, will be accepted by Him Who knows how impossible it is for the sufferer to make any mental effort.

Except for confession and surrender there is nothing else we can do. Many have a feeling that

they are not worthy to receive so great a gift, and
wonder if they ought not wait before seeking it.
What should we wait for ; can we make ourselves
more worthy ? No, it is because of our unfitness
in soul and body that we need to come to the
Saviour. We must come to Him just as we are,
to let Him make us what He would have us to
be. The only thing we can do is to surrender
ourselves to Him. The very faith in which we
pray; and in which we come to Him for healing,
is His gift.

The only reason for delay, and one that I often
recommend, if the need for healing is not impera-
tively urgent, is to enable the mind to become
more expectant. To many, who have not realized
that Christ is still the Healer, the idea of coming
to Him for healing is too new, too good to be true ;
and even after the truth has been accepted, time
is sometimes needed for the truth to become established sufficiently to enable the sufferer to come
with real expectation.

Suppose now that you are ready to seek healing.
If you are confined to bed, or unable to leave the
house, you must send for the " Elders of the Church,"
and ask for Ministration. Sadly we must admit
that it is not every parish priest who is ready to
minister the Healing Sacrament of the Church ;
though I believe that many more would be led to
do so, if they received calls from the members of
their flock. If your parish priest will not come,
you must seek farther afield ; and if you do not

know of any one who can help you, a letter to the
Secretary of one of the Guilds of Healing would be
the best step to take.

If you are able to get about, and can find no help
in your own locality, there are Services of Healing
held from time to time in London and in different
parts of the country. If you are going to seek
healing at one of these Services, or going to receive
private Ministration, do regard the matter with due
seriousness. If the healing is so much desired, it
is worthy of sacrifice. The day appointed for the
Ministration should be a day set apart for that
purpose alone, a day dedicated to God. It is all
very well to fit in a visit to the dentist with a day's
shopping, or between two social engagements; but
not a visit to a " Healer," because you are not going
to the " Healer," you are going to Christ. We
must remember that it is for His Glory that we
should seek healing, and therefore it is not a matter
to be treated lightly, as something we can do when
we have a suitable opportunity, and are not too
busy with our own affairs. My own experience
is that those who find healing most readily are
those who are willing to put themselves out in the
quest for it.

Having come to the time of Ministration, fix your
thoughts on Christ, and on Him alone. Think not
of the infirmity from which you seek deliverance,
but of the perfection which you know is His will
for you. Think not of the man who is ministering
to you; but believe that Christ Himself, Who has

no visible Hands to-day, is using the hands of His
Minister as if they were His own. Believe that you
are verily and indeed receiving a Gift of Grace, the
free Gift of God ; not depending upon any possibility of worthiness in yourself, but upon the Passion
of our Lord ; not depending upon any ability to
feel the reception of the Grace, but upon the promise
of Christ Himself. You are coming in the Name
of Jesus, daring to use His Name because He has
redeemed you. In His faith, because the faith you
have, is the power of His Spirit within you ; and
therefore you can claim the fulfilment of His
promise. If you could see Him standing before
you, there would not be any shadow of doubt ; and
is He not truly present, although His Presence is
not visible ?

In the upper room at Jerusalem on the night
before His Passion, our Lord said to His Disciples :
" A little while, and ye shall not see Me ; and again
a little while, and ye shall see Me." This, the
Authorized Version, fails to reveal the true meaning,
as it gives no indication of the fact that Christ used
two different words, which are both translated
" see." The Revised Version makes the meaning
clearer by translating it thus : " A little while, and
ye behold Me no more ; and again a little while,
and ye shall see Me." If we substitute the word
" perceive " for the word " see " we get the real
meaning. " A little while, and ye behold Me no
more (in the visible body) : and again a little while,
and ye shall perceive Me (spiritually)." Though
the bodily form would be no longer visible, they

would have a spiritual assurance of His abiding presence. Again He said: " It is expedient for you that I go away." Were they to imply from that nothing more than that His presence in the Spirit would free Him from the limitations of time and place imposed upon a bodily presence ? Surely He meant that His continually abiding presence in the Spirit would be even more real to them than His bodily presence had been ; and the fellowship in the Spirit more close, more satisfying even, than the fellowship under the old conditions. I cannot believe that six months after the Day of Pentecost, any of the Apostles would have desired to return to the old conditions, at the cost of losing the Spiritual fellowship which was so manifested in their lives and conduct. Are we then to envy those who had faith because they saw Jesus with their eyes, when He has given to us the power to have an even more perfect realization of His presence ?

Pray, therefore, that the Holy Spirit will give you the instinctive realization that you are kneeling before Christ Himself, and there will be no room for fears or doubts ; you will know that you are receiving the Gift of His Grace : and, knowing that you have received, you will give thanks naturally and spontaneously.

If surrender is absolutely complete, the only reason that can prevent instantaneous healing is our inability to expect it ; and of that I have written in another chapter. I have no doubt that this statement will be questioned by many, and I

shall be told that healing is often delayed in order
that some lesson may be learned more thoroughly.
Such cases should surely be classed as those where
absolute surrender is not complete ; and I base my
statement on the fact that, when Christ was on
earth, no healing was delayed for more than a few
moments, for the purpose of strengthening the
suppliant's faith. We are far too ready to attribute
the results of human weakness to some hidden
purpose of God ; just as the doctrine of the
Church was changed, somewhere about the tenth
century, when the Church, having lost power
to heal, began to teach that sickness was sent
by God as part of life's discipline. The only
time that the will and purpose of God could
be perfectly manifested was when Christ was on
this earth ; and we have no right to declare
that His will and purpose have been altered,
when we are unable to give Him the conditions
necessary for such manifestation. I am not blam-
ing any individual for being unable to expect
instantaneous healing ; the inability is one of
the products of the long neglect of the Ministry
of Healing, and the progress of a civilization
which binds us more and more to the material
things of life. No doubt many are disappointed
when instantaneous healing is not manifested ;
they were so sure that they really did expect
it. It is quite easy to mistake a very strong
hope for faith ; or to think that, because the
conscious mind seems to be confident, all will
be well. But we forget the lurking fears in

the subconscious mind, and the atmosphere of
doubt surrounding us. There are several ways
in which the reality of the expectation can be
tested.

How much trouble are you prepared to take, or
how much inconvenience are you prepared to suffer,
in order to obtain healing? I have known people,
who would not hesitate to pay any price for surgical
or medical aid, grudge the expense of putting themselves in a position to receive Divine Healing. To
such an one the seeking could only be experi-
mental.

Again, what is your outlook for the future? If
you are seeking healing from some weakness of the
eyes; have you such assurance, that you are prepared to break up, or give away, your glasses, before
receiving Ministration; or do you think it would
be wiser to wait, and see if you can do without
them? If you have to wear some special kind of
boot, which would be useless if your foot, or leg,
were as they should be, would you, like the case
mentioned by Mr. Hickson, go to the expense of
buying an ordinary pair of boots, and take them
with you to the Healing Service, convinced that
they would be necessary for your return journey?
If the Service were within walking distance, but
your infirmity necessitated the use of some conveyance in order to reach the place, would you, or
not, make arrangements for the same conveyance
to take you home again? You may say, " But
how can I be sure that it is God's will for me to be
healed instantaneously? " Because Christ is " the

same yesterday, to-day, and for ever"; and if you could know that you were coming to the visible Christ you would have no shadow of doubt whatever.

"Why," you may ask, "if God is so loving, and so anxious to deliver us from all evil, does He not manifest His power, even if we are unable to come in full expectation?" I cannot take it upon myself to answer that question, but I can suggest two possible reasons. If every one, who came to seek healing through the ministry of the Church, were to receive full and instantaneous healing, God would be condoning the existing standard of faith in the Church. The fact that so many healings are delayed is surely a stirring call to the Church to seek to raise the standard. The other reason I suggest is, that as I believe that God works through the mind to the body, the doubts lurking in the mind are actually preventing the manifestation which the Father is so willing to give.

Suppose now that you have received Ministration. If there is already visible or perceptible result, all is well; but if there is neither, do not be disappointed. The seed has been sown, there can be no doubt about that; so you will at once give thanks, and pray that nothing will hinder the growth. Praise God day by day; even if the infirmity shows as yet no signs of giving way. Nothing brings us nearer to God than praise. Even in thanksgiving we cannot always get away from

" self," because we naturally thank Him more
spontaneously for the things which please us,
than for those which are displeasing, though
in reality they may be more profitable. Even
when we are praying for other people, " self "
comes in, because we naturally pray more earnestly
for those who mean most to us. But when we
praise God for what He *is*, and not merely for
the benefits we receive from Him, " self " has
no place, and we are lifted up to the plane
upon which He is able to manifest His Glory
in us.

Do not be surprised, or dismayed, if things seem
to go badly after you have received Ministration.
In the war, whenever our soldiers made an advance,
they had to " dig in " under fire. So when we
strive to make an advance Spiritually, we are
challenging the enemy ; and he is not slow to accept
the challenge. Do not be frightened ; the powers
of darkness cannot hurt us, except on their own
plane. If we trust the Holy Spirit to keep us on
the Spiritual plane, they can do us no more harm
than the sharks in the sea can do to the passengers
on the deck of a ship.

Moreover, if we want to live by faith we must
be prepared to have our faith tested. It would be
easy enough to have faith if everything were to go
smoothly. The test is to hold on in spite of trial :
to stand fast by the promises of God, in spite of
outward appearances. We want a faith which is
equal to all the attacks which can be made upon

it ; so the Father allows it to be tested, in order that it may be strengthened.

The seed which has been sown is good seed, it is for us to see that it is sown in good soil, and well watered.

CHAPTER IX

FAILURES

WE have still to face the fact that there are many earnest Christians who have sought healing from God in all sincerity of faith, but have not recovered their health : the so-called failures, which sceptics delight in bringing forward, as evidence against the truth of Divine Healing.

I admit the difficulty, as it is useless to close one's eyes to facts ; but I would point out that a great many cases of delayed healing are counted as failures by impatient observers. We must be very careful how we judge a failure. You may give up a certain kind of medicine because it is obviously having no effect ; but if you are seeking healing direct from God, though you may have been to all the teachers, and have read all the books, without any apparent improvement in your condition, you have not, and never will in this life, come to the end of the teaching of the Holy Spirit ; nor has He ceased to work in you, so how can you say that healing will not come ?

Though I do not pretend to be able to explain anything like all the cases in which the healing has not been manifested, I am perfectly convinced that the failure is not on God's side, but on the side of humanity. In saying this I am not casting the blame on any individual. Far be it from me to say that any particular individual could have been healed, if he, or she, had had more faith, or had been more obedient to the will of God : but when we remember the foundation of our faith, *i.e.* that Christ upon the Cross did bear the burden of our sicknesses, as well as the burden of our sins, it must be admitted that God has done all that could be done to make healing possible for every one of His children.

We certainly do not believe that it is God's will that any one should remain in a state of sin, yet there are many failures to realize the full redemption from sin. There are many who have humbly confessed their sins to God, sincerely desiring to amend their lives, who have undoubtedly received full and complete absolution from the sins of the past, who still have to come to God repeatedly for forgiveness of the very same sins committed again and again. You may argue that it is human nature ; and that no man can expect to be entirely without sin. That may be true ; but you must admit that if we could surrender ourselves so completely to God, that He could fill us with His Holy Spirit, we could not sin : the Holy Spirit within, ruling every thought, word, and deed, would make sin impossible. St. John in his first Epistle (chap. iii. verse 6) assures us that " Whosoever abideth in Him sinneth not." We have got into the way of regarding sin as inevit-

able, because so few have been taught to look to
the power of the Holy Spirit to keep us from sin.
The doctrine of regeneration has been taught freely
but not the doctrine of sanctification, although it
figures so largely in the teaching of St. Paul. No
doubt even those who live closest to our Lord frequently make mistakes which need to be confessed
as sins, but no professing Christian ought to be
content, until every sinful desire has been rooted
out of the heart by the power of the indwelling
Spirit. Till we have reached this state we have
to confess that the same sins do defeat us time after
time, and we label them " besetting sins."

Now take the case of a really devout person
sincerely and constantly trying to overcome a
besetting sin, but having failed so often that he
begins to regard the struggle as hopeless. It would
never occur to any of us to suggest that the fact of
that sin being still in evidence was the proof that
it was God's will for it to remain. We know that
it only remains because the victim has been asking
God to help him face the temptation, instead of
praying that the Holy Spirit would root the desire
for it out of his heart ; and then trust to Him for
protection.

Of course it cannot be God's will for any sin to
remain, for sin in any form must be abhorrent to
the All-Holy God, Who gave His only Son to redeem
us from the power of evil.

In face of the fact that the Bible proves so clearly
that sickness is evil in origin, and that the burden
of it was borne for us by our Lord upon the Cross,

what justification have we for supposing that a
disease, which remains unhealed in spite of persistent prayer, is in accordance with the will of
God? It can only mean that somewhere on
the human side there is a failure to fulfil the conditions under which God can manifest His healing
Love.

In the case of sin, we do not hesitate to admit
that the failure must be on our side; why then
should we be so unwilling to admit the same of the
sickness; and prefer to accept the continuance of
it as a proof that God has altered His purpose, or
fails to keep His promises?

The problem of the unhealed has caused various
learned writers on the subject to put forward a
theory that, although there is no doubt about the
general truth of the Healing Gospel, there seem to
be exceptions, and that some are called upon to
endure patiently the diseases which afflict them.
There is nothing in the Bible to justify this theory,
except the misinterpretation of St. Paul's thorn;
nor can they comfort the sufferer by quoting any
Beatitude for the patient bearing of sickness. The
sufferer can only strive to seek consolation in the
idea of sharing the sufferings of our Lord, who was
untouched by sickness; or of being made perfect
through suffering, by ignoring the fact that suffering
for that purpose must be voluntary.

Why not face the facts boldly, and accept the
teaching of the Bible that there are only two reasons
for unhealed sickness, *i.e.* want of faith, and disobedience? I do not mean that I would advocate

going to a sick man and bluntly accusing him of
either. The lack of faith may not be his fault;
and the sickness from which he is suffering may be
the result of the sins of his fathers, rather than of
any particular sin of his own.

It is not easy for the faith of an individual to rise
far above the level of the faith of his friends, so
before we can blame any friend of our own for lack
of faith, let us test the progress we are making.
We ought to find the fullest faith among those who
are keen enough about Divine Healing to be members
of a circle praying for the sick. Suppose that we
are members of such a circle, and that some one
relates to us the story of some very remarkable case
of healing. What is the word which will rise to
the lips of probably the majority of the hearers?
I have generally found it to be the word " Wonderful," and the tone of voice indicates that it is an
expression of surprise, rather than of adoration of
our Lord. If our faith were what it ought to be,
should we be surprised? All God's works are
wonderful; but faith should not show surprise at
the perfect answer to prayer.

A lady, who was suffering from some complaint,
was invited by some friends, who believed in Divine
Healing, to go to stay with them, so that they might
help her by their prayers. She accepted their
invitation; and on the third morning of her visit
she awoke entirely free from pain. She arose, and
went to join her friends at breakfast, telling them
the good news that she was healed. They would

not believe her! The very people who had been
praying for her, and who had invited her to their
house for that very purpose, could not be persuaded
to believe that their prayers had been answered!
Before we are too critical, let us remember that even
the stout-hearted Christians, who were spending the
night in prayer for St. Peter in prison, would not
believe that it was he himself knocking at the gate.

It is not only difficult for the faith of the individual
to rise above the level of the faith of his friends,
but it is also difficult to rise above the level of
popular expectation. Certain things are taken for
granted, and expected by all, such as the knitting
together of the broken bone: others are regarded
as impossible. It is by no means easy for the
individual to escape from the influence of the " mass
mind "; in fact it is impossible for most people to
do so, till they have the personal experience of the
Living Christ. Even where there is strong faith in
ultimate healing, the effect of the generally accepted
opinion of mankind is evidenced in the almost
unconscious classification of diseases. One finds it
almost taken for granted that certain diseases, or
conditions of mind, or body, will take much longer
to heal than others, which are generally considered
less severe; and yet what a simple matter the
healing of one of our little bodies must be to the
Almighty Creator of the Universe.

There is no doubt that many remain unhealed
because of the faithlessness of relatives and friends.

I have known it happen on several occasions ; in fact it was such a case that led me to see the advantage of a Home of Healing, in which sufferers could escape from an atmosphere of doubt. This wrong atmosphere is very often caused by love, strange as it may sound. The patient, too ill to pray for himself, is surrounded by those who love him so dearly that they cannot bear to think of the possibility of losing him. This naturally causes anxiety, and those who ought to be the channels of healing Grace are so full of fear that, not only are the channels blocked, but their fears are imparted to the sick man himself, thus raising a barrier of fear and doubt which prevents the healing love of Christ from reaching the one who would otherwise have been restored to health.

The general unbelief of the Church is undoubtedly the greatest barrier of all, especially as this unbelief is so widespread among those who are ordained to be the ministers of Christ's Healing—to heal the sick is one of the charges given to a Bishop at his consecration.

It is all very well for the clergy to argue that their first duty is the spiritual welfare of their people ; and that the souls of men are more important than their bodies ; or that they are so busy with the Spiritual work of the parish, that they have no time to attend to the bodily needs, which are the care of the doctor.

It is the generally accepted part of the duty of the Parish Priest to visit the sick, and I can testify from my own experience how much more satisfying such visits can be, in spreading the joyful message of the healing Christ, and ministering to the sick, instead of having nothing to offer except exhortations to bear, as patiently as possible, the sicknesses which we were taught to believe were sent by the God who is Love.

The neglect of the Ministry of Healing is not only disobedience to the Master's command, but it has also weakened, beyond conception, the power of the Church to reach the masses who regard the Church as having no message for them.

Can we not see also, that in neglecting the Healing Ministry, the Church has lost the most valuable touchstone of faith. When the Church found her power to heal disappearing, she changed her doctrines to suit her failure, instead of searching for the weakness in herself, which was causing the failure. When Christ was on earth, the Healing Love of the Father was manifested through His perfect body. His visible body to-day is the Church. If the Healing Grace cannot flow freely to-day, or at any other time, it must be because the body is an imperfect channel. How glorious would the faith of the Church have been to-day if for nineteen centuries she had applied this test, and humbled herself before God whenever the waning of her power to heal convicted her of some wrong within ! With what power she might have gone out to win the world for Christ, stirring men by the healing of their bodies to seek the greater blessing of the healing of their souls. Think what it would have meant in the Mission

Field, where the childlike simplicity of the native so readily accepts healing. And yet men will not believe that the work, which occupied so large a place in the Ministry of Jesus, is an essential part of the work of His Church to-day.

Without a doubt our greatest hindrance is the want of faith of the Church; but before we blame the Church, we must remember that it is composed of individuals; and the standard of faith of the body cannot be higher than the average level of the faith of its members. Are we accepting what we find, and grumbling about it; or are we trying to raise it? We have no right to grumble if we are making no attempt to raise it.

If the power to heal is the test of the soundness of the Visible Body of Christ, ought we not regard power to receive healing as the test of the moral soundness of the individual. It is a very solemn thought, and one we must not refuse to face; though of course we remember that unsoundness need not necessarily mean wilful sin; it may also be caused by fear, or ignorance, or a mistaken conception of God's purpose. Inasmuch as sickness is essentially evil, and no evil can exist where the Spirit of God is in complete possession, the presence of disease must indicate that there is something that needs to be surrendered, or some lesson that God requires us to learn, before His Spirit can have entire control of soul and body: and failure to obtain healing is a stern challenge to submit our whole being to His scrutiny.

We have seen that the inability to expect great things makes great things impossible So much more does fear of failure, or disaster, tend to bring about the very things we are afraid of.

Fear is not only the cause of many illnesses, but also prevents many from being healed. It is not surprising that a patient, whose bodily infirmity tends to produce infirmity of mind, should find it difficult to escape from a fear which is almost universal, such as, for instance; the doctor's pronouncement that he is suffering from a disease which is generally recognized as incurable. Such fear can only be overcome by faith in the Living Christ.

Many chronic complaints are maintained by fear. As soon as symptoms are observed there is a fearful expectation that they will lead to the results which experience has led one to expect. A sore throat is expected to be the forerunner of a cold, and sure enough the cold develops in due course. Moreover, the fear need not be consciously apprehended. Let the same sequence of events happen a few times and a thought track is established in the subconscious mind, which only needs the acceptance of a suggestion to set it in motion, even though the acceptance may not have been accompanied by any conscious fear at the time. For instance, if a person has become convinced that sitting in a draught always results in catching cold, it is quite sufficient for the mind to realize that there is a draught, even though the attention may have been too much occupied to be conscious of fear, and the thought is set in motion.

Many failures are due to the fact that, though a a patient has been healed from some disease, he has not sought protection from the fear of it, and is therefore quite likely to be watching anxiously for any symptoms that might suggest its return. Under such conditions the return is more than probable, and the reality of Divine Healing is called in question.

Fear being really the failure to believe implicitly the promises of God, failures through fear come under the heading of want of faith; so again we see the need of the personal experience of realizing the Living Christ; and belief that the Holy Spirit can make the Truth of God live in our hearts. But faith will not develop if we do not act it. If I get the symptoms which threaten the coming of a cold, special efforts of prayer will not hinder its development; for the simple reason that the fact that special efforts are deemed necessary is an acknowledgment of fear, and tend to strengthen it. If, on the other hand, I can ask simply for protection, and then, casting fear aside, make up my mind that it does not matter, that I am quite content to leave myself in the Hands of God, in complete indifference as to whether I have a cold or not, all is well. I have never had a cold develop when I have been able to do this. If you are called upon to come in contact with any infectious or contagious disease, do not pray that you will not take it, for that would be to acknowledge fear. Pray rather that you may be delivered from *the fear* of taking it ; and then leave yourself in God's keeping.

Having given so much attention to the serious consequences of fear, it is quite possible that I may be raising a fear of fear itself ; so before proceeding I would like to try to show the way in which it can be overcome.

If a fear has become persistent, or recurrent, it means that it has become a fixed idea in the subconscious mind, and cannot therefore be destroyed by the power of the will. We must look to God for deliverance, and pray that the Holy Spirit will drive out the fear. This must be done reverently, and decidedly. First a definite prayer, then a waiting in the silence, followed by thanksgiving, because you know that your prayer has been answered. Now comes the test of faith. The thought will come back. If you are going to be disappointed, and possibly rather aggrieved, because you really did believe that it would disappear, you will simply deliver yourself into its power again : but if you face it with boldness, regarding it as a temptation, affirming that you know that it can no longer hurt you, it will soon fade away. There is a very great difference between regarding it as a thought that has not yet gone, and one that has been driven out, but is trying to come back. If you look upon the fear as not having yet gone, even though you are confident that it will go some day, you may wait indefinitely for it to disappear. If, on the other hand, you believe in faith that your prayer was answered, and the fear driven out, you will be able to regard it merely as a temptation to fall back again into the old condition. Resist the tempter, and he will flee from you, and the fear will have no power to hurt you. If you have several fears disturbing your peace, do not start by seeking deliverance from the biggest first, however anxious you are to be rid of it. We get help in proportion to our ability to expect; and it is much easier to expect deliverance from a small fear, than from one which has been dominating you for a long time: but when you find that the lesser fears are being driven out, your faith will become strong enough to expect deliverance from the greater. I have known of a fear, great enough to wake its victim in a perspiration of terror, completely driven out, long before the cause of it was taken away.

Sometimes failure is due to too much knowledge. It is much more difficult for one who understands the gravity of a disease, and the usual process of development, or the physical changes which have to take place before healing can be accomplished, to have the simple childlike faith of one who has no such knowledge. This is the reason why instantaneous healing is more frequent among primitive peoples, and children, than among educated people. Again, it is really want of faith; the acceptance of man's wisdom, and the conditions of the material world, in preference to the promises of God.

Some failures are due to the fact that there is more of self-effort than of simple trust. In cases of long-delayed healing there is often the feeling on the part of the patient that there is something more that he ought to do ; so he makes various attempts, such as trying a different method of prayer, or longer periods of devotion, or more frequent Communions. All these are excellent in themselves, but useless, if carried out with the idea of *winning* healing. Healing cannot be *won*, it must be accepted as God's free gift ; and as in the case of all His gifts, our part is, having prayed for them, to act as if we have received, rather than to strive to obtain them.

I have known failures through inability to give up the discussion of symptoms. Even the careful recording of progress, and the desire to talk about it, keeps the thought of the disease fixed in the mind, and so retards healing. How frequently Christ told those whom He had healed, to go and tell no man ; because He knew that the continual recital of the symptoms which had been taken away, even when talked about with the intention of bearing witness, would keep the mind filled with the thought of the disease, and so cause the return of it.

The majority of people are much too fond of talking about sickness, and discussing with one another their symptoms and their ailments. They little realize the harm they are doing by thus keeping the mind filled with thoughts of infirmity, instead of thoughts of health. We are often told that the mischievous or desperate deeds some youngsters commit are due to the influence of the cinema. Their minds are so filled with the exploits of desperadoes, that they seem unable to control themselves. Let those who seem to gloat over the discussion of diseases take care lest they find the thoughts of the mind manifesting themselves in the body.

It may sound a strange statement to make ; but I believe it is true to say that some of the most puzzling cases of failure are due to the " Spirituality " of the patient. A spiritually minded person, who has, in all probability, been brought up to regard sickness as part of God's discipline, and the body as unworthy of too much attention, is naturally inclined to accept sickness as a cross, and to feel that patient endurance can be offered to God as the sacrifice of self. This attitude might also be encouraged by the misunderstanding of St. Paul's thorn ; and failure to realize the fact that Christ bore the burden of sickness upon the Cross. If the body is the Temple of the Holy Spirit it cannot be unworthy of attention ; and it certainly cannot be vile, since the Son of God deigned to use it ; though no one would suggest that it is equal in value with the soul.

Once again I would urge that the suffering we offer to God must be voluntary ; and a suffering that we have tried to get rid of cannot be counted as that, simply because we have been unsuccessful in our attempt. When, however, that offering has been made in all sincerity of belief, even though we know the belief to be mistaken, I cannot think that it has not been accepted in the spirit in which it has been offered : in fact the beauty of character sometimes developed by such patient suffering is surely a proof of acceptance. For all that, the greater Glory of God would have been manifested in healing, if it could have been accepted. Does it sound hard to say " if it had been accepted," as though there had not been many earnest prayers for healing, before the infirmity was counted to be the will of God ? What I mean is that, though the prayers may have been earnest enough, if there was a doubt about God's will, they were not prayers of accepting faith.

Again, faith may be weak because of age. The patient may get the idea that he is too old to have the right to expect healing, and in any case he must die some day. God can withdraw the life He has given, when He will ; He does not require the body to be destroyed by disease ; and as far as age is concerned I have not yet discovered that at which healing can be no longer expected. I once ministered to an old lady of seventy-six, suffering severely from rheumatism. She had not been out of doors for many months, and was unable to raise her arms to the back of her head. Four days after she had been anointed, she went for quite a long walk ; and a few days later was able to do her own hair without assistance. Once I was called to see an old man of seventy-eight, on, what was expected to be, his death-bed. I saw him two years later sawing up logs !

The length of life is in God's keeping, and it is not for us to attempt to interfere ; but disease is

an evil thing, and we have the right, nay, the duty,
to seek deliverance from the evil, quite apart from
the question of the length of life. If I could know
for certain that it was God's plan to call one of His
servants home to-morrow, it would not lessen my
efforts to seek healing for him to-day, praying, not
for longer life—that is for God to decide—but that
he might be delivered from all evil, in soul and
body.

In quite a number of instances I have seen the
healing granted within a few days of the passing of
the soul : it can never be too late to pray that God
will glorify Himself by delivering one of His children
from the power of evil.

The other cause of failure, according to the
teaching of Scripture, is disobedience, or sin. We
have already considered the necessity of seeking the
cleansing of the heart, as well as the healing of the
body ; so that if the body remains unhealed we
must pray that the searching light of the Spirit of
Truth will show us if there is still some sin which
has not yet been purged away.

In some cases the failure to obtain perfect health
is due to the sin of not seeking healing for the Glory
of God, and therefore not desiring complete healing
We have all probably heard some one say, " If I
can get rid of the pain I will put up with the inconvenience." We have no right to tolerate anything
that defiles the Temple of the Holy Spirit.

You would be surprised to find how many there
are who do not want to get perfectly well. Most of
them are quite unaware of this, and often very

difficult to convince, because when they were really ill they were sincerely desirous of being healed. They fail to realize that, when the severity of the illness has passed, the desire for complete healing is overshadowed by reluctance to forgo all the little cares and attentions to which they have become accustomed.

Again, many are quite proud of having something the matter with them, especially if it is something out of the ordinary. It is the old sin of vanity, which makes them hold on to anything which stamps them as being a little different from other people, and brings attention which they would not otherwise receive. There is also the fact that human nature does like to have an excuse for failures, and bodily infirmity is so satisfying, because it is a genuine excuse—if the infirmity is real—and not merely a case of neurotic imagination.

I am afraid that you may think that there are so many difficulties in the way, and matters to be observed, that healing through the Grace of God is too difficult to attempt. Do not be discouraged; in reality nothing could be more simple, provided that we desire to be right with God. The difficulties are those we make for ourselves, in our lack of simplicity; and the desire to examine the revealed Truth of God in the light of our own reason, instead of accepting it as God's Word. The Truth is sim licity itself. It is the Will of God the Father to deliver His children from every manifestation of evil, in soul and body. He is the Fountain of all Healing.

Jesus Christ is the Channel through Whom the Father's Healing Love flows out to us. The Holy Spirit is the Power of God working in us to manifest the Healing Love of the Father, which faith in Christ, and Christ alone, enables us to receive.

EPILOGUE

THE scene is the study of an English country Rectory.

There enters a young girl, limping and in pain; she has twisted her ankle in the road, and has been brought home in a neighbour's car.

The Padre asks her, " Do you believe that if you could see Jesus standing here He would heal you ? "

" Yes, sir," answers the girl.

" Do you believe that Jesus is here, though you cannot see Him ? "

" Yes, sir."

" Do you remember that Jesus told His Disciples to lay hands on the sick in His Name : that is to say that, though He has no Hands that we can see He can use my hands to heal you ? "

" Yes, sir."

A short prayer is offered, claiming His promise—in His Name, because He has redeemed us ; in His Faith, because His Spirit is within us. Hands are laid upon her head, followed by thanksgiving, and the girl walks out of the study to continue her usual occupation.

Could anything be more simple, when childlike faith accepts the promise of the Father's Love, through Jesus Christ our Lord ?